Collins

.on Book 2

Your Life

The whole-school solution for PSHE and Citizenship

Mya Rai   8c

John Foster and Simon Foster

William Collins' dream of knowledge for all began with the publication of his first book in 1819. A self-educated mill worker, he not only enriched millions of lives, but also founded a flourishing publishing house. Today, staying true to this spirit, Collins books are packed with inspiration, innovation and practical expertise. They place you at the centre of a world of possibility and give you exactly what you need to explore it.

Collins. Freedom to teach.

Published by Collins
An imprint of HarperCollinsPublishers
The News Building
1 London Bridge Street
London
SE1 9GF

Browse the complete Collins catalogue at
www.collins.co.uk

10 9 8 7 6 5 4 3

ISBN 978-0-00-759270-8

John Foster and Simon Foster assert their moral rights to be identified as the authors of this work.

British Library Cataloguing in Publication Data
A Catalogue record for this publication is available from the British Library.

Commissioned by Letitia Luff

Managed by Caroline Green

Edited by Vicky Leech

Designed and typeset by Jordan Publishing Design Limited and eMC Design Ltd

Copy-edited by Donna Cole

Proofread by Cassandra Fox

Indexed by Jane Henley

Cover design by Angela English

Cover photograph Dudarev Mikhail/Shutterstock

Production by Rachel Weaver

Acknowledgments

The publishers wish to thank the following for permission to reproduce photographs. Every effort has been made to trace copyright holders and to obtain their permission for the use of copyright materials. The publishers will gladly receive any information enabling them to rectify any error or omission at the first opportunity.

(t = top, c = centre, b = bottom, r = right, l = left)

Cover Dudarev Mikhail/Shutterstock, p6 Simone van den Berg/Shutterstock, p8 Piotr Marcinski/Shutterstock, p9 Monkey Business Images/Shutterstock, p10t ejwhite/Shutterstock, p10b Luis Carlos Jimenez del rio/Shutterstock, p11 lady.diana/Shutterstock, p12 Sergei Bachlakov/Shutterstock, p13 Tad Denson/Shutterstock, p14t Eric Gaillard/Corbis, p14b Featureflash/Shutterstock, p14c Mark Makela/Corbis, p15 muzsy/Shutterstock, p17 dboystudio/Shutterstock, p18t Dragon Images/Shutterstock, p18b 6348103963/Shutterstock, p20t Birgit Reitz-Hofmann/Shutterstock, p20b Rob Marmion/Shutterstock, p21t hans.slegers/Shutterstock, p21b Creatista/Shutterstock, p22 bikeriderlondon/Shutterstock, p23t Maxisport/Shutterstock, p23b Media24/Gallo Images/Getty Images, p24 Istvan Csak/Shutterstock, p26 g-stockstudio/Shutterstock, p27 wavebreakmedia/Shutterstock, p28 prudkov/Shutterstock, p29 Creatista/Shutterstock, p32 Tootles/Shutterstock, p33 Alexander Trinitatov/Shutterstock, p34t Stone36/Shutterstock, p34b 13/James Whitaker/Ocean/Corbis, p35 Creatista/Shutterstock, p36 Twin Design/Shutterstock, p37 Odua Images/Shutterstock, p38 UIG/Getty Images, p39 pcruciatti/Shutterstock, p40t photo.ua/Shutterstock, p40b Martynova Anna/Shutterstock, p41 pcruciatti/Shutterstock, p42 spirit of america/Shutterstock, p43 Rimantas Abromas/Shutterstock, p44l Tetra Images/Getty Images, p44r Frank F. Haub/Shutterstock, p45 Mert Toker/Shutterstock, p46 enciktepstudio/Shutterstock, p47 mangostock/Shutterstock, p48 Olga Rosi/Shutterstock, p49 Monkey Business Images/Shutterstock, p50 Stuart Monk/Shutterstock, p51 Alan Bailey/Shutterstock, p52 dboystudio/Shutterstock, p53 iev radin/Shutterstock, p54l Arieliona/Shutterstock, p54r Yuriy Rudyy/Shutterstock, p56 auremar/Shutterstock, p58 John Gomez/Shutterstock, p59t bibiphoto/Shutterstock, p59b wavebreakmedia/Shutterstock, p60 Aletia/Shutterstock, p61 g-stockstudio/Shutterstock, p63l Stuart Monk/Shutterstock, p63r Stokkete/Shutterstock, p64 Monkey Business Images/Shutterstock, p65 Francis Wong Chee Yen/Shutterstock, p66 Monkey Business Images/Shutterstock, p67r Dragon Images/Shutterstock, p67l luminaimages/Shutterstock, p68 Alexander Raths/Shutterstock, p70 pedrosala/Shutterstock, p71 jennyt/Shutterstock, p72 YanLev/Shutterstock, p73 Ivan Roth/Shutterstock, p74 Simone van den Berg/Shutterstock, p75l Joshua Resnick/Shutterstock, p75r Dudarev Mikhail/Shutterstock, p76 solominviktor/Shutterstock, p77l Aleksandar Mijatovic/Shutterstock, p77r Pressmaster/Shutterstock, p78 Martin Novak/Shutterstock, p79 wavebreakmedia/Shutterstock, p80 Dan Kitwood/Getty Images, p81 WPA Pool/Getty Images, p82 WPA Pool/Getty Images, p83 Paul Hackett/Corbis, p84 Christopher Elwell/Shutterstock, p85t Eddy Galeotti/Shutterstock, p85b Claudio Divizia/Shutterstock, p86 Christopher Elwell/Shutterstock, p87 Anthony Shaw Photography/Shutterstock, p88 stockyimages/Shutterstock, p88–89 Yuganov Konstantin/Shutterstock, p89tr Martin Good/Shutterstock, p89tl JuliusKielaitis/Shutterstock, p91 ndoeljindoel/Shutterstock, p92 Duncan Andison/Shutterstock, p93 Taina Sohlman/Shutterstock, p94 Monkey Business Images/Shutterstock, p95 from Dorset Echo/Newsquest Media Southern Ltd, p96 Groundwork, p97 Corepics VOF/Shutterstock, p98 Budimir Jevtic/Shutterstock, p99 Brian Eichhorn/Shutterstock, p100 auremar/Shutterstock, p101l Daniel M Ernst/Shutterstock, p101r Daniel M Ernst/Shutterstock, p102l tukkata/Shutterstock, p102r nodff/Shutterstock, p103l muratart/Shutterstock, p103r Aleksandar Mijatovic/Shutterstock, p104 Gajus/Shutterstock, p105 Fisherss/Shutterstock, p106 41941/Shutterstock, p107t Martchan/Shutterstock, p107b spwidoff/Shutterstock, p108 paulaphoto/Shutterstock, p109 Blend Images/Shutterstock.

Contents

Your Life Student Book 2 is the second of three books which together form a comprehensive course in Personal, Social and Health Education (PSHE) and Citizenship at Key Stage 3. The table shows how the topics covered in this book meet requirements of the National Curriculum for Citizenship at Key Stage 3 and provide a coherent course in PSHE for students in Year 8.

Personal, Social and Health Education

Personal wellbeing – Understanding yourself and handling relationships	Social education – Responsibilities and values	Keeping healthy
These units concentrate on developing your self-knowledge and your ability to manage your emotions and how to handle relationships.	These units concentrate on exploring social issues and on developing an understanding of your responsibilities towards other people in society, your values and your opinions.	These units are designed to help you take care of your physical and mental health.

- **You and your feelings**
  – self esteem

- **You and your time**
  – making the most of your leisure

- **You and your family**
  – divided families

- **You and other people**
  – friends and friendships

- **You and your achievements**
  – reviewing your progress

- **You and your responsibilities**
  – other cultures and other lifestyles

- **You and your values**
  – where do you stand?

- **You and the community**
  – the school as a community

- **You and your opinions**
  – speaking your mind

- **You and other people**
  – older people

- **You and your body**
  – drinking and alcohol

- **You and your body**
  – contraception and safer sex

- **You and your safety**
  – at home and in the street

- **You and your body**
  – drugs and drugtaking

The various activities within each unit provide opportunities for you to learn how to grow as individuals, for example, by developing self-awareness and taking responsibility for keeping healthy and handling your money. The group discussion activities involve you in learning how to work as a team and how to develop the skills of co-operation and negotiation. You are presented with situations in which you have to work with others, to analyse information, to consider moral and social dilemmas and to make choices and decisions.

Citizenship

Becoming an active citizen	Economic and financial capability
These units focus on the society in which you live, on its laws and government and on developing the skills you require to become an active citizen.	These units aim to help you to manage your money effectively, to learn about the world of work and to practise the skills of being enterprising.

- **You and the law**
  – the police

- **You as a citizen**
  – Britain's government

- **You and global issues**
  – food and water

- **You and the community**
  – taking action

- **You and your money**
  – making the most of your money

- **You and your money**
  – gambling

- **You and the media**
  – the power of advertising

- **You and the world of work**
  – employment and unemployment

- **You and the world of work**
  – understanding business

Self-esteem and confidence

Self-esteem

What is self-esteem?

Self-esteem means having a good opinion of yourself. It is based on understanding what your strengths are and valuing yourself as a person.

Why is self-esteem important?

Self-esteem is important because it enables you to have the confidence to be yourself. If you have self-esteem, you will say what you think and do what you think is right, rather than say or do things to try to impress other people.

Having self-esteem will make you feel happier. You won't let people make you feel badly about yourself if they criticise you unfairly. Because you believe in yourself, you'll respect yourself and other people will respect you too. You won't fall into the trap of blaming yourself for everything that goes wrong in your life.

Self-esteem will give you the confidence to try new experiences. It will also help you to achieve more, because you will have a positive attitude that makes it easier to deal with setbacks.

Is having self-esteem the same as being conceited?

No. A conceited person has an exaggerated opinion of themselves. A person with self-esteem has a balanced view of their own worth, valuing their good points, but understanding that, like everyone else, they are not perfect.

Feeling confident

Some people seem to be born confident. They can enter a crowded room, immediately feel at home and settle down and talk to anybody. Confidence comes from believing in yourself and feeling happy. Once you're confident about what you want out of life, you can go for it.

When you're confident about yourself – how you look and how you feel – many other problems disappear. Perhaps you have to read some of your work out in front of the whole class. If you feel confident in yourself, you'll be less pre-occupied with things that don't matter – like how you look and where you're sitting – and more concerned with making the reading interesting for the rest of the class.

In pairs

On your own, make one list of the things you are good at, and another list of the things you think you're not so good at. Then show your lists to a partner. Go through the list of good points and discuss the things you've included that make you feel good and that you are most proud of. Then choose one of the things from your not-so-good list and discuss together something positive that you could do in order to get better at it.

Know yourself

Make a list of what your strong points are. You can feel proud of what you're good at.

Good points	Not-so-good points
making friends	tidying room
swimming	getting to sports practice on time
telling jokes	
eating healthy food	handwriting
studying hard	cleaning shoes
organising games	nail biting
painting	brushing hair
staying fit	washing dishes

Erica Stewart **offers tips on how to build up your self-esteem**

Think positively

Look at things in a positive rather than a negative way. For example, if you do badly in a test, don't think: 'I'm hopeless. I'm never going to get a good mark.' Instead, think about what you can do to make sure you get a good mark next time, such as asking for extra help with things you don't understand.

Stand up for yourself

Make up your own mind about what you believe and stick to it. It's harder to say no than to say yes, but don't let anyone pressurise you into doing things you don't believe are right. Don't feel guilty or that you're letting them down. You'll respect yourself far more for sticking up for your beliefs than if you give in and do something just to please others, and other people will respect you more, too.

Be realistic

Be realistic about what you can achieve. Don't set yourself unachievable targets. If you're really determined to do something, then go for it. Adopt a step-by-step approach, setting yourself a series of short-term goals and dates by which to achieve each one.

Cope with criticism

If you're criticised, it can damage your self-esteem. Consider carefully whether the criticism is fair. For example, if you let the rest of the cast down by not turning up for an important play rehearsal, then accept that it was your fault. Apologise and reassure everyone that you won't let it happen again. But if you are being unfairly criticised, recognise what is going on and either ignore it or take steps to ensure that it doesn't continue.

Take risks

If you're not prepared to take risks then you cut down on the chances of having new experiences and finding out what you're capable of doing and achieving. Of course, that doesn't mean doing things that are dangerous or reckless. But avoiding taking any risks because you're afraid of making a fool of yourself won't do anything for your self-confidence. It's usually best to have a go. If it doesn't work out, you can always tell yourself that at least you tried.

In groups

Discuss the advice that Erica Stewart gives in her article. Which piece of advice is the most useful? Which is the hardest to put into practice?

Study the six statements below. Talk about each one in turn, saying why you agree or disagree with it. Make notes of your views and share them in a class discussion.

1 What other people think of you and your behaviour is more important than what you think yourself.

2 It's not being conceited to feel proud of yourself and your achievements.

3 It's not what you look like that matters, it's what kind of person you are and how you feel about yourself.

4 If you're not confident about doing something, it's better to avoid doing it rather than risk making a fool of yourself.

5 People who keep putting you down only do so to try to make themselves feel better.

6 Imitating people by doing whatever is regarded as cool and trendy is the best way to boost your confidence.

Shyness

Coping with shyness

Few people are strangers to shyness.
It sweeps over us in many situations: arriving at a party, talking in front of the class, starting a conversation with someone important or taking on a new task. Even something as 'simple' as ordering gig tickets over the phone for the first time or signing your name at the bank can make you feel awkward.

Shyness, one of the most complex and untalked about emotions, has many different effects. Dry mouth, fumbling, stuttering, avoiding eye contact, not speaking up, blushing, feeling sick, sweating, headaches: it's no wonder the word most often coupled with shyness is 'crippling'. It can stop you accepting invitations, trying new experiences and getting on in life.

As a teenager you are at the peak of your self-consciousness, and shyness is a result of worrying about your image. You are looking and feeling different, experiencing new emotions and being put in more 'adult' situations. You want to deal with situations smoothly even though you've never encountered them before.

As you become older and more experienced a lot of the awkwardness you feel goes away.

But you can help yourself now by recognising that the way you feel reflects your own thoughts. If you're down on yourself – 'No one likes me'; 'I look awful'; 'I never know what to say' – you are bound to feel shy.

How to beat shyness

- Shy body language can make situations worse. **Try to speak clearly** (mumble and you will be asked to repeat yourself) and look people in the eye.
- **Think positive.** Tell yourself you can cope and you will. Try and focus on what you like about yourself and what you are good at. For example, if you are a good skater, imagine yourself skating confidently.
- **Taking a deep breath** and relaxing will stop your mind working overtime. If your body is calm, you are less likely to fluff your words.
- Shy people are often seen as 'aloof' or 'off' because they stand alone and look unapproachable in social situations. Try to **break the ice** before your anxiety builds up, and don't put on a front.
- **Be realistic.** Just because you are feeling self-conscious doesn't mean everyone is looking at you or analysing your every word. Look at the situation rationally and realise that you are not the centre of attention.
- **Face the fear.** If you are scared of doing something, do it anyway. It's the only way to learn.

In groups

Discuss what you learn about shyness from the article on this page. Talk about what causes shyness and how it makes you feel.

Discuss the advice given on how to cope with shyness. Which do you think are the most useful of the tips?

Coping with classroom
MISTAKES X

Embarrassment and fear of failure can hold you back from contributing in class. However, not speaking out has far-reaching effects outside the classroom. It can stop you standing up for yourself and your beliefs, and it can make you miss opportunities. If you let the fear of failure (the fear of getting something wrong or saying something embarrassing) overwhelm you at school, it will overwhelm you in everything you do.

The things to remember are:

X It's not the end of the world if you give an incorrect answer.

X Not understanding something isn't a sign of stupidity. But not asking for help is foolish.

X Embarrassment is usually only momentary.

X No one remembers the things you get wrong.

X Speaking in front of people gets easier the more you do it.

X If someone shouts you down, assert yourself and ask them to let you finish.

Making mistakes

Making a mistake can not only be embarrassing, but it can also damage your self-confidence. Everyone makes mistakes. So when you make a mistake, it's important to keep it in perspective and to learn from it.

Learning from your mistakes

- Growing up is all about experiencing things for the first time. It is easy to make a mistake when you are inexperienced.

- If you make mistakes because you are careless, try to give more time to things. Take life more slowly. Think things through and plan how you're going to act.

- If you think you might make mistakes because you feel uncertain or ignorant about something, talk about it with someone you trust. Don't act without a second opinion.

- If you make mistakes because you're nervous, take a deep breath before you act. Don't panic yourself into acting on impulse or in a way which isn't really you, just because you think you must make your mark.

- Concentrate on all the good things you can do, and don't dwell on things you aren't so good at. Making mistakes is all about lacking knowledge – and that's something you can work on putting right.

Don't blame yourself

- If you blame yourself for everything that goes wrong, you'll soon begin to lose confidence in yourself.

- But everybody makes mistakes. It's part of human nature. If you can learn from where you went wrong, you'll become a wiser person.

In groups

1 Talk about how to cope with classroom mistakes. Is it fair to make fun of people who make mistakes in class?

2 Discuss the advice on learning from your mistakes. What do you think is the most useful piece of advice?

For your file

Use the information in this unit as the basis for a short article for a teen magazine, explaining why it is important to have self-esteem and what you can do to build up your self-confidence.

Drugs – facts and fictions

> Many young people who start taking drugs don't realise what they are getting into. There are lots of myths about drugtaking. Before you do anything rash, it's worth knowing all the facts and what risks are involved.
> *– Drugs counsellor*

Fact or Fiction

Only other people get hooked or hurt by drugs

Part of the problem with drugs is that most users think they're invincible. They believe that the dangers will never affect them because it's other people who end up being rushed to hospital, other people who can't handle the effects of drugs.

If you're someone who is tempted to take drugs, don't ignore the information and warnings. Drugs can and do kill. They don't discriminate – it could happen to anyone.

Fact or Fiction

People get their drugs from pushers

Contrary to popular belief, most people come into contact with drugs through friends and older siblings, not through anonymous pushers on the street. What's more, being approached by someone you like makes saying 'no' harder and more complicated.

Fact or Fiction

All drugs are dangerous

The danger when taking drugs depends on many things, such as *what* you've taken, *how much* you've taken, and your *state of mind* at the time. Although some drugs are less dangerous than others, illegally manufactured drugs are *always* a danger because it's impossible to tell what's in them. Never trust a friend who tells you something is safe because they've tried it. Everyone reacts differently to drugs – body size, weight, age and sex all affect the kind of reaction a drug will create.

Fact or Fiction

Soft drugs lead to hard drugs

One of the greatest myths surrounding drugs is that taking soft drugs automatically means you'll end up on hard drugs. There is no evidence to suggest that this is true, although taking any kind of drug does increase your chances of coming into contact with harder drugs. This is because drugs like Ecstasy, Speed and LSD are often mixed with other substances, and are often available through the same sources. What you have to remember with drugs is that you always have a choice. A choice not to take them, a choice to stop taking them and a choice not to go any further.

Is cannabis safe?

You may have heard people say cannabis is risk-free. This isn't true.

- Heavy use of cannabis over a long period of time can lead to users relying on the drug as a way of relaxing and being sociable.

- **Heavy, long-term cannabis use can make you feel less energetic than normal. This can have a negative effect on the way you live your life.**

- Smoking cannabis with tobacco causes lung damage. In fact it's reckoned that smoke from an unfiltered spliff carries more risks than a cigarette. However, people tend to smoke many more cigarettes than spliffs.

ECSTASY FACTFILE

Name: The chemical name for ecstasy is MDMA.

Form: Ecstasy comes as tablets of different shapes, sizes and colours. Because it can look like many other drugs or medicines, a lot of people have been sold tablets that have turned out not to be ecstasy. As you can never be quite sure what you are buying, a lot of people think buying ecstasy isn't worth the risk.

Legal category: Ecstasy is a Class A drug. It is illegal to possess or supply Ecstasy.

Effects: Ecstasy is a stimulant that users say gives them a 'rush' feeling followed by a sense of calm, making them feel closer to other people and more aware of their surroundings. They get an energy buzz, which means they can dance for long periods. The effects begin about 20 minutes after they've taken a tablet and last for several hours.

Risks: As Ecstasy starts to work, the user sometimes feels sick, their heart rate increases, and their jaw muscles tighten. Some people become anxious and feel confused and frightened.

Ecstasy raises the body's temperature. Dancing for a long time in a hot atmosphere after taking ecstasy can lead to overheating and dehydration (loss of too much body fluid). The risks can be reduced by 'chilling out' and taking regular breaks from dancing, and by drinking about a pint of a non-alcoholic fluid, such as water, fruit juice or a sports drink every hour. Users are advised to sip the drink regularly, to avoid alcohol, and to eat salty food in order to replace the sodium they have lost through sweating.

Once the effects of the ecstasy wear off, users can feel tired and depressed, but may find it hard to sleep.

Research into the long-term effects of using ecstasy suggest that heavy use may cause damage to the brain, leading to depression and memory loss later in life. Use of ecstasy has also been linked to liver and kidney problems.

There are around 50 deaths a year as a result of taking ecstasy. Evidence suggests that most are caused by heatstroke.

For your file

Use the information on this page to write an article for a teen magazine entitled 'Ecstasy – is it worth the risk?' Explain what physical effects ecstasy has – both pleasurable and harmful – and give your views on the risks involved in taking Ecstasy.

In groups

What have you learned from these pages about the risks of drugtaking? Discuss the views of these young people (below) and say why you agree or disagree with them.

"*Experimenting with drugs is too risky. You don't know what you're taking and how your body will react.*"

"*There's too much fuss about drugtaking. Most people who take drugs get a good feeling and it doesn't do them any harm.*"

"*Taking drugs is a waste of money. You don't need drugs in order to have a good time.*"

In pairs

Study the article on ecstasy. Make a list of the most important facts about ecstasy you've learnt from the article.

Role play

Act out a situation in which a doctor explains to a teenager the risks involved in taking ecstasy and smoking cannabis.

Role play a scene in which two people argue about the risks of drugtaking – one saying it's worth the risk, the other saying it's not. Take it in turns to be the person saying that it's not worth the risk.

Drugs and the law

If the police have reason to suspect you're carrying an illegal drug, they have the right to make you turn out your pockets. They can also take you to the police station and search you. If drugs are found, you could be charged with one of TWO offences.

1 Possession

This means being caught with an illegal drug for your own use. The police can tell your parents or carer. They could also inform Social Services and the Probation Service. As for punishment, the police can give you either a reprimand, a warning or prosecute you (see page 39). If you are found guilty in court you can get a fine or a custodial sentence.

2 Possession with intent to supply drugs

If you had any intention of dealing (which can include giving and sharing drugs), you may be charged with this more serious offence. Decisions over whether you're charged with intent to supply are based on the circumstances in which you were caught and the quantity of drugs you were caught with. The police can take the same course of action as in simple possession cases, but this time you're more likely to be charged. If your case goes to court the penalties are likely to be heavier.

If you have a drugs record:

● Obtaining a visa to travel to some countries may become difficult or could even be denied.

● It could also affect your job prospects. When you're applying for a job, an employer may check if you have a criminal record or any past convictions.

The Misuse of Drugs Act divides drugs into three classes and gives guidance for appropriate penalties.

Class of drug	Types	Maximum penalties
Class A	cocaine, crack, ecstasy, heroin, LSD (acid), magic mushrooms prepared for use, speed (amphetamines) if prepared for injection	**Possession:** 7 years' prison and/or unlimited fine **Supply:** life imprisonment and/or unlimited fine
Class B	cannabis, speed (amphetamines)	**Possession:** 5 years' prison and/or unlimited fine **Supply:** 14 years' prison and/or unlimited fine
Class C	rohypnol, supply of anabolic steroids and tranquillisers, possession of temazepam (mazzies)	**Possession:** 2 years' prison and/or unlimited fine **Supply:** 14 years' prison and/or unlimited fine

In groups

Discuss what you learn from this page about the laws on drugs.

1 What can the police do if they think you are carrying drugs?

2 If you are caught carrying drugs, what offences could the police charge you with?

3 What are the different classes of illegal drugs? How do the maximum sentences differ according to the class of a drug?

4 What are the possible consequences of having a drugs record?

5 How effective do you think the current drugs laws are? Do you think they act as a deterrent? What effect do you think they have on the way drugtakers obtain and use drugs?

6 Do you think the drugs laws should be changed in any way? Should there be harsher penalties for supplying drugs?

7 What are the arguments for and against making drug use legal and allowing people to possess drugs in small amounts for their own personal use?

For your file

Write a statement giving your views on the drugs laws.

Saying 'no' to drugs

In groups

Talk about all the different situations in which a teenager might be offered drugs. Why might they choose to refuse or accept? Talk about factors that might influence their decision, such as where they are, who they are with, what mood they are in and how much pressure is put on them to join in.

Discuss the advice in the extract on how to turn down drugs and stay friends. Which piece of advice do you think is the most helpful?

Role play

Role play a scene in which a teenager is being offered drugs and a group of their friends is putting pressure on them to accept. Discuss various tactics that the teenager can use in order to say no. Is it best to just say no and walk away? To state clearly the reasons why you personally don't want to take them? To argue with the people who are offering them to you, and try to stop them taking any?

Take it in turns to be the person being pressurised, and discuss which of the tactics worked most successfully.

How to turn down drugs and stay friends

▶ Say no and don't feel bad about it. Obsessing about what you've said, how you've said it, and what people think of you is unhelpful.

▶ Being the only non-drug taker may feel awkward and uncomfortable but this is just a phase and, like most phases, it will pass.

▶ Don't make things worse for yourself by letting your imagination exaggerate a situation. Being the 'odd one out' is hard but it doesn't mean your friends no longer like you.

66 *When I refused to smoke drugs at a party, I worried that all my friends thought I was being stupid. I got so upset about it that I went home early and cried. Over the weekend I decided that if they didn't like me for not taking drugs, I wasn't going to be friends with them any more. When I got to school on Monday, I was all ready to fight with them but then I found out they were all worried about me and had no idea why I'd got so upset.* **99**

▶ Most of the time no one is judging you. Everyone is so worried about themselves and how they look to other people that they aren't even thinking about you.

▶ Question people who try to bully you into taking drugs. After all, if drugs are so brilliant, why is it so necessary for them to have your company? If someone is giving you grief for saying no, ask them the following:

➡ Why is it so important for you to take them?

➡ Why are they so stressed out about you saying no?

➡ Why do they have to make other people take them too?

Britain
a diverse society

Today, Britain is a diverse society consisting of people from many different ethnic backgrounds. This is due to the large number of immigrants who have come to live in Britain over the last 60 years.

During the 1950s and 1960s, large numbers of people came to Britain from the Caribbean and South Asia. Immigration was encouraged during these years because workers were needed to help rebuild the British economy after the end of the Second World War.

More recently, there have been large numbers of immigrants from Poland and several other eastern countries that joined the EU in 2004. An estimated 2.33 million people who were born in other EU countries were living in Britain in 2011. This included 521,000 people from Poland, and Polish is now the second most common language spoken in Britain.

The 2011 census showed that 14% of the population of England and Wales came from ethnic minorities. The largest number were Asian/Asian British (7.5%), followed by Black/African/Caribbean/Black British (3.3%) and mixed/multiple ethnic groups (2.2%).

In Scotland and Northern Ireland, ethnic minorities make up a much smaller percentage of the population.

The ethnic minority population is currently concentrated in the larger cities, such as London and Birmingham, and in particular smaller cities such as Leicester and Bradford.

According to research carried out at Leeds University, the increase in the number of people from ethnic minorities living in Britain will continue to rise in the future.
It predicts that ethnic minorities will make up 20% of the UK population by 2051 compared to 8% in 2001.

People from ethnic minorities have introduced their own cultures and lifestyles to Britain. Members of their communities have made significant contributions to society in all walks of life – industry and commerce, medicine and science, politics, the media, arts and sports.

Businessman Stelios Haji-Ioannou

Politician Baroness Warsi

Pop star Rita Ora

In groups

Discuss what you learn from this page about ethnic diversity in Britain today.

Ethnic stereotyping

It is important not only to respect other people's cultures and lifestyles, but also not to discriminate against them by stereotyping them. **Ethnic stereotyping** means thinking that all people from the same ethnic background have similar characteristics and behave in exactly the same way.

❝I was singing an Asian song, and my best friend – she's Afro-Caribbean – said, 'Don't tell me you're one of those?' I said to her, 'One of what?' She replied, 'You know, TP,' and I asked her, 'What's TP?' She said, 'Typical Paki.' I answered her, 'So what, I'm proud of who I am.❞
– Nazrah

❝My friend Asif's a really good footballer. But lots of the other kids say he'll never get anywhere because there's this idea that Asian boys haven't got what it takes to become professional footballers.❞ – Tariq

In groups

1 Discuss Nazrah's comment. Are young people from ethnic minorities sometimes stereotyped because of the music they like? Are people sometimes stereotyped because of the way they dress?

2 Discuss Tariq's comment. Then read and discuss John Agard's poem 'Stereotype'. Talk about the stereotypical views that people have of what people from different ethnic groups are good at doing.

3 Talk about national stereotypes, for example, the views that other people sometimes have of English people as either stiff, cold and unfriendly, or as aggressive, beer-drinking football hooligans. What stereotypes are there of **a)** Scottish, **b)** French, **c)** German people? Discuss how these stereotypes have come about and why they present a false image.

Stereotype

I'm a fullblooded
West Indian stereotype
See me straw hat?
Watch it good

I'm a fullblooded
West Indian stereotype
You ask
if I got riddum
in me blood
You going ask!
Man just beat de drum
and don't forget
to pour de rum

I'm a fullblooded
West Indian stereotype
You say

I suppose you can show
us the limbo, can't you?
How you know!
How you know!
You sure
you don't want me
sing you a calypso too
How about that

I'm a fullblooded
West Indian stereotype
You call me
happy-go-lucky
Yes that's me
dressing fancy
and chasing woman
if you think ah lie
bring yuh sister

I'm a fullblooded
West Indian stereotype
You wonder
where do you people
get such riddum
could it be the sunshine
My goodness
just listen to that
steelband

Isn't there one thing
you forgot to ask
go on man ask ask
This native will answer
anything
How about cricket?
I suppose you're good at
it?

Hear this man
good at it!
Put de willow
in me hand
and watch me stripe
de boundary

Yes I'm a fullblooded
West Indian stereotype

that's why I
graduated from Oxford
University
with a degree
in anthropology

John Agard

Images and stereotypes

Ethnic minorities still shown as stereotypes in films, says study

Films are perpetuating harmful out-of-date stereotypes of black people, says a new study.

Forty per cent of those surveyed said black characters don't get enough 'good guy' roles, and over 50% believe black characters are too often portrayed as drug dealers.

One in three said roles for minority groups often have little depth and are poorly written. Just under half believed that Asian characters are too often portrayed as having family conflicts.

Eastern Europeans are shown as being ill-educated and at the bottom of the economic ladder – a new potential stereotype.

From a report in the *Guardian* 18 March 2011

In groups

1 Discuss what is meant by negative stereotyping. Talk about how ethnic minorities are portrayed in recent films you have seen. Are they still stereotyped?

2 Do you agree that TV programmes fail to reflect real life and are guilty of tokenism? What are the arguments for and against including scenes showing racism?

3 Talk about recent TV programmes and films that have featured people from ethnic minorities. Discuss how the characters were portrayed and whether or not you think they were stereotypes.

4 Choose a popular TV soap, and share ideas for introducing two new characters from an ethnic minority background. Discuss how you would integrate them into the story in order to present a true picture of what life is like for people from their background in Britain today.

TV programmes don't reflect real life

TV programmes are criticised for their portrayal of ethnic minorities. Although Eastenders has included Asian characters since 1985 and Coronation Street got its first permanent Asian family in 1998, both programmes have been accused of stereotyping ethnic minorities.

Ethnic minority viewers accuse broadcasters of tokenism and of screening exaggerated and extreme representations of minorities and failing to reflect real life. It is argued that they present a false picture of society, in which everyone shows each other tolerance and respect; whereas if they reflected reality they would include scenes showing some characters being casually racist or making racist remarks behind closed doors.

A distorted picture?
Does the media stereotype Muslims?

Do TV and newspaper reports present a stereotyped picture of Muslims living in the UK? According to Dr Awad, an Imam in Liverpool and a professor of Islamic studies, the media has now created a stereotype of Muslims.

"Everyone thinks we are all terrorists but this is not the case. This is partly due to the individual behaviour of some Muslims who have been brainwashed and fuelled by hatred. But we condemn this behaviour. This is not the way of Islam! This is against the teachings of the Qur'an! But the media has led people to believe this is what Islam is all about."

The media is also accused of giving a false picture of Muslim women as 'uneducated' and 'oppressed' and forced to wear the veil. But whether or not a woman wears the veil is a matter of choice and many Muslim women are well-educated with successful careers.

"The media fails to include good news stories about Muslims. How often do you see a story about a successful Muslim?"

"I have been called a terrorist in the past and sometimes people assume that, because you are wearing a hijab, you are oppressed.

It can be difficult to fight stereotypes but you brush it off. It is just people being ignorant. We live in a society where everyone is different so it is important people understand each other so we can live in harmony together."

Mariam Rafa, 16

The Press

What people read in the newspapers can also influence how they think about other social groups, including ethnic and racial minorities. If, for example, people from India are always presented as poor, starving or the victims of drought, that creates a false picture of Indians in general, even though it is right to report the human tragedies. Newspaper readers may never get to hear about the Indian scientists, writers, entrepreneurs, film-makers, artists and engineers.

Young, gifted and black

How often do you see a news story about young black people's achievements? A recent study found that nearly 70% of news stories published about black young men and boys related to crime.

Campaigners argue that the media should show more examples of young black people achieving success, for example at school or in business, so that there are more visible positive black role models.

In groups

Discuss Mariam's comments. Do you think the media stereotypes Muslims?

Study some recent editions of either a national newspaper or a local newspaper. Discuss the reports and articles they carry about people from ethnic minorities. What images of them do they convey? Do you think they present a true picture of what their lives are like and the contribution they make to society?

For your file

What do you think newspapers should be doing to make sure that they do not reinforce stereotyping? Write an e-mail either to a national or local newspaper saying what you think the editor and staff should be doing to make sure that they do not stereotype people in their paper.

Needs and wants

The things we spend money on can be divided into two groups

First, there are the essential things we need to be able to survive – necessities. These include our homes, the electricity and gas we use to heat and light them, the water supply we have, the food we eat, the clothes we wear to keep warm, and the toiletries such as soap and toothpaste we buy to keep ourselves clean and healthy.

The second category of things we spend money on are things we want to have – luxuries. These make our lives more comfortable, such as fridges to keep our food fresh, telephones so that we can keep in touch with families and friends, bicycles and cars so that we can travel, and personal computers. This category also includes the money we spend on entertainment either at home on TVs, DVDs and computer games, or outside the home on going to the cinema, to clubs, to sporting events and on holidays.

In groups

Study the list of all the things your parents or guardians might spend money on and decide which are necessities and which are luxuries. Add any other items you can think of to the list.

Discuss which items are regular expenses and which are weekly, monthly, quarterly or annual payments. Which are variable expenses because they are one-off payments?

Include items such as mortgage repayments/rent, utility bills (electricity, gas, water), council tax, food, clothes, telephone calls/line rental, TV licence or subscription, transport (bus fares, petrol, car tax, car insurance), lottery tickets, newspapers/magazines/books, household cleaning items, flowers, cinema/concert tickets, school uniform, school trips, presents, holidays, gym/sports club membership, pocket-money.

Now make a list of all the things you spend your money on and decide which are necessities and which are luxuries.

In pairs

Discuss which luxuries are the most important to you and which you would be prepared to do without in order to save money.

Petra's Problem

Petra doesn't think she's particularly extravagant. She's got three special friends and they enjoy hanging out together. So when she's not with them, she likes to keep in touch with them and she's always either texting them or chatting to them on her mobile. They go into town together on Saturdays and Petra often can't resist buying herself something new. She likes to keep up with all the gossip about her favourite bands, so she buys a magazine too. Because she likes music, she regularly downloads new tracks onto her iPad. She enjoys dancing and goes to a dancing class. But she's always short of money, so she's thinking of giving it up, even though the dance teacher says she's one of the best in the class.

For your file

Write a paragraph offering Petra advice on how she could manage her money, so that she can continue with her dancing class.

How to make money – increasing your income

Ian Ashendon offers advice on how you can increase your income

As well as cutting down on your expenditure, you can increase your income by investing your savings. You can also make money by working, or selling items you no longer want.

Invest your savings

Don't just keep the money that you are saving in a piggy bank. Pay the money into a bank or building society each week or month. Look for a savings account that will pay you a good rate of interest. That way you are less likely to dip into it if you find yourself suddenly short of cash.

Find a job

There are various jobs that a young person can do to make money. It may involve you giving up part of the weekend or getting up early. It may even be boring and repetitive. But you need to keep positive and to remind yourself that if you want something in life you must be prepared to make sacrifices and to work for it.

Among the jobs young people can do are:

- Chores for your parents, such as mowing the lawn, cleaning the car or vacuuming the carpets. It may be that you can negotiate a pocket-money rise in return for doing extra chores.
- Babysitting for relatives or neighbours.
- Helping an older person by doing jobs they find difficult, such as carrying groceries, heavy lifting or sorting out simple problems they are having with the computer.
- Taking dogs for walks or looking after pets for neighbours who may be unable to do so, because they are ill or away from home.
- A paper round or helping a stallholder at a local market or an event, such as a car boot sale.

Whatever work you do, it is important to be punctual, polite and reliable.

Sell items you no longer want

You may be able to make some money by selling items that you no longer want. You can put an advert in a local shop window, sell items on the internet, or take items such as DVDs or games to a shop that will accept them either in part-exchange or will give you cash for them.

Some tips about selling

- Only sell things that you own personally. Don't sell things that are shared by the family – unless you have the permission of your parents, brothers or sisters.
- Be careful of selling things on the internet. Make sure you only use sites that are safe and secure and that can offer protection for buyers and sellers.
- Don't sell items at school. It's usually against the school rules.
- Don't try to sell items that are damaged or don't work properly without making it clear to the buyer that they are not in perfect condition.
- Don't overprice an item. Find out what the item is worth by researching how much other people are charging for a similar item, then set a fair price that you are willing to sell the item for.
- Be prepared for the buyer to try to bargain with you. You may, therefore, want to set an asking price that is slightly higher than the price you are willing to accept.
- Make sure that the buyer pays for the item before you hand it over. If necessary, let them try it out to check it works, but make sure they don't take it away without giving you the money, even if you are selling it to a friend.
- If you are made an offer and are unsure whether or not to accept it, say you'll think it over. Then ask an adult you trust what they think you should do.

In groups

Discuss the advice Ian Ashendon gives about finding jobs to earn money. Which of his suggestions do you think is the most helpful? Share your experiences of doing jobs to increase your income.

Discuss the advice on selling items. In your experience which is the best way to sell unwanted items – by putting an advert in a shop window, at a car boot sale, on the internet, or to friends? Do you agree with the advice Ian Ashendon gives?

Top Tips

Making the most of your money

Erica Stewart explains how to make the most of your money

✔ Follow the 80/20 rule

However much money you get from your parents, grandparents or other sources, always follow this rule. Only spend 80% of your weekly or monthly income on your needs and wants. Put the other 20% aside for savings. By following this rule, you'll always have the back-up of a savings account that you can dip into when you have extra expenses, such as birthday presents you need to buy or spending money that you want for holidays.

✔ Set yourself realistic goals

For example, if you want to buy yourself a new mobile phone, work out how much money you will need to save and how long it will take you to save it. Be realistic: don't choose a model that is beyond your means. Work out what is affordable on your income.

✔ Skip going out every time you are asked

If you really want something, be prepared to give up something so that you can save towards it. This may mean not doing something you'd really like to do. But at least you'll have the satisfaction of knowing that you are making a real effort to increase your savings.

✔ Do a deal

If you show that you are really making an effort to save money yourself, you may be able to do a deal with your parents or some other close relative. Perhaps you have a birthday coming up and they will agree to pay half the cost if you save up the other half.

✔ Research before you buy

Make sure you are getting the best value for your money, especially if you are buying a big item. Find out all you can from reviews in magazines or on websites about the quality of what you are buying and the reputation of the manufacturer. Talk to people who are knowledgeable about the product and who you can trust to give you an honest opinion.

Go into different stores and check online to compare prices. See where you can get the best deal. Comparison shopping can often result in big savings. You may also be able to take advantage of special offers, store coupons or vouchers.

✔ Take care of what you buy

Look after your gadgets, especially if they are expensive. You don't want to have to pay for the same item twice. Also, if at some time in the future you want to upgrade to a newer model, then you will get a better price for an item that is in good condition than if you had not looked after it.

✔ Avoid impulse buying

Whenever you go shopping, have a clear idea of what you plan to buy. If you are going shopping to help a friend choose a new item of clothing, don't be tempted into buying something for yourself when you hadn't planned to do so.

✔ Set yourself a spending limit

If you are planning to buy something for yourself, set a spending limit before you go out and stick to it. Don't be tempted to go over your limit or to buy something else that you see instead which costs more.

✔ Keep tabs on your spending

Keeping a check on what you are spending is important. It needn't be time-consuming or complicated. Simply, keep a notebook and write down everything you buy each week. Set aside a regular time for doing it each week, so that it becomes a habit. By looking at the pattern of your spending, you can then make changes, for example, if you discover you are spending too much on snacks and magazines.

✔ Don't lend money that you can't afford to lose

When a friend asks you to pay for them to do something or to borrow money from you, think carefully before you agree. Are they always short of money? Will they be able to pay you back? Can you do without the amount of money they want? Never lend money that you can't afford to lose – even to your closest friend.

✔ Don't borrow money that you can't afford to pay back

Think carefully before you borrow money. Will it create a problem for you in the future? Will you be able to pay it back? Would it not be better to wait until you had saved up the amount yourself? When you borrow money, you are agreeing to give away part of your future income. Don't borrow money that you can't afford to pay back.

✔ Don't rely on your parents to help you out

You aren't being fair to your parents or yourself if you rely on them for handouts when you have overspent. Good money management skills are essential if you are going to get the most out of your money.

In groups

Discuss each piece of advice in turn and give it a mark out of 10, according to how useful you think it is. Decide which three pieces of advice your group thinks are the most useful and share your views in a class discussion.

5 You and your values

What influences how you behave?

The way you behave is influenced by your beliefs and values. For example, in some situations your behaviour might depend on how important you think it is to impress people, compared to doing what you believe to be right.

What plays the most important part in influencing how you behave? Here are some possibilities. On your own, rank them in level of importance on a five-point scale – 1 for extremely important, 5 for not at all important.

Trying to avoid arguments

Standing up for what you believe is right

Making sure your actions don't hurt other people

Trying to impress people

Listening to what your parents and teachers say

Keeping out of trouble

Doing what your religion says you should do

Keeping your temper

Following the latest fashion

Behaving with courtesy

Telling the truth

Looking after your own interests

Imitating the behaviour of your idols

Respecting other people's opinions and beliefs

Keeping your promises

Doing what your friends want you to do

Your ambitions

What you believe to be important, and what your values are, will influence your ambitions.

Here is what a group of young people said when asked what their ambitions were:

"To make money."
"To get married."
"To have a satisfying career."
"To live a long life."
"To contribute to the community."
"To have people's respect."
"To travel the world."
"To become famous."
"To make the most of my talents."
"To have children."
"To help other people."
"To be happy."
"To keep fit and healthy."

In groups

Compare how you have ranked the things that influence your behaviour and discuss what you think the most important influences should be.

In groups

Study the list of things young people said were important to them when asked to think about their ambitions. Add anything else to the list that you think is important. Then decide on the five most important things to you and talk about why you think they are important to you.

Idols or heroes?

by Derek Stuart

Everyone has famous people that they look up to and admire, but are they idols or heroes?

Many teenagers, when asked who they admire most, give the name of a film star, a pop singer, a TV celebrity or a sports star. These people certainly have talent and are often good-looking. Many of them have worked hard and shown determination to achieve what they have. They are rich and famous and have exciting lifestyles. But are they really heroes?

The way I see it, a hero is somebody who has shown exceptional qualities. They are people like Nelson Mandela, who was prepared to go to prison to fight for his rights. They are people who are prepared to risk or sacrifice their lives for other people. They are people who achieve things against the odds and who set an example to us all by the way they behave.

So when I'm drawing up my list of heroes for my hall of fame, I'm looking beyond the stars of stage and screen, playing field and catwalk, to those exceptional human beings whose behaviour has been truly heroic.

In groups

Discuss what Derek Stuart says in his article about the difference between idols and heroes. Do you agree with him? What do you think is the difference between an idol and a hero? Together, decide what your definition of a hero is.

Draw up a list of people you consider to be heroes who your group would put in their 'hall of fame'. Draft a short statement explaining your reasons for including each person. Then present your views in a class discussion and agree on a class list of 'Our Top 20 Heroes'.

Someone you admire

Think of someone you know personally and admire for some reason: perhaps because of what they have achieved, the way they behave towards other people or the courage and determination they have shown in difficult circumstances. It could be a relative, a friend of the family or a neighbour.

Study the list below and pick out the qualities that make you admire them:

> *intelligence   tact   courage*
> *determination   selflessness*
> *tolerance   cheerfulness   patience*
> *generosity   loyalty   reliability*
> *kindness   sympathy   creativity*

In pairs

Take turns to discuss the person you most admire and why.

Cause for concern

The eight reports on these two pages all appeared in the *Daily Express* on Thursday 31st of January 2013. Which of the issues described in the reports do you think is the most important?

A

It's a dog's life without any meat

By Geoff Maynard

Two-thirds of British dogs are not fed meat as part of their daily diet, researchers claimed yesterday.

Six per cent have never eaten meat – and a quarter of owners admit they have never given their dog a bone.

Instead, many people give their pet treats like crisps, cheese and cake, according to a poll of 2,000 dog owners. Yet, a third admit their dog prefers meat. Clare Scanlon of Butcher's Pet Care, which carried out the poll, said: "Dogs are carnivores. With this move away from a natural diet we are killing them with kindness. No wonder dog obesity is on the rise."

B

The six hours a day telly addicts

by **Nathan Rao**
Consumer Affairs Editor

Britain is a nation of telly addicts regularly spending a quarter of the day glued to the box, new research reveals.

A study by YouView showed one in four viewers watches up to six hours of television a day.

The poll of 2,000 adults also found that a quarter of Britons use social media while watching television, regularly tweeting or posting updates throughout programmes.

Viewing habits vary between the sexes, with women watching more television than men.

C

Dementia drug gives new hope

by Jo Willey

A new dementia drug is showing significant promise in clinical trials, according to research.

The daily jab of Cerebrolysin improved brain function in sufferers.

The review published in The Cochrane Library brought together the most up-to-date evidence on the treatment for vascular dementia – the second most common form after Alzheimer's.

Dr Eric Karran of Alzheimer's Research UK, said: "Vascular dementia affects thousands in the UK, but sadly there are no specific treatments available for people with the condition. Research into new treatments is absolutely vital."

D

Migrants shun the English language

by Sarah O'Grady

More than four million migrants in Britain cannot or rarely speak English.

In figures showing the stark impact of years of mass immigration, one million barely use English, with a staggering 138,000 unable to utter a word of it.

The findings, released by the Office for National Statistics, show how much the face of the UK has changed with a patchwork quilt of languages covering the country. In some areas up to four out of ten people only speak English as a second language.

Last night experts warned of the potential damage to local communities and one said: 'Those who want to live in Britain should make an effort to learn English.'

E

Marathon girl's death linked to sports stimulant

by David Pilditch

The grief-stricken boyfriend of marathon runner Claire Squires demanded urgent action to save lives yesterday as it was revealed she died after taking a popular sports supplement.

Claire put a scoop of the supplement, called Jack3d, in her water bottle before last year's London Marathon to give her an energy boost if she 'hit the wall', an inquest heard.

She had no idea the product she had bought online contained an amphetamine-like stimulant with potentially lethal side-effects.

Claire, an experienced marathon runner, collapsed with a massive heart attack as she approached the finishing stretch near Buckingham Palace.

F

Foreign aid cash is 'wasted'

Millions of pounds of taxpayers' cash is at risk of being squandered in the government's dash to meet its overseas aid spending targets, senior MPs warned today.

The Commons International Development Committee said ministers should be prepared to miss overseas development aid targets rather than waste cash.

Chairman Sir Malcolm Bruce said MPs were worried pressure to increase aid could lead to poor spending decisions by the Department for International Development.

H

Tobacco smuggling spivs 'rob taxpayer'

by David Craik

One in four cigarettes in the UK is being sold on the black market, Imperial Tobacco revealed yesterday as it warned smuggling would hit its profits, fund crime and take away vital government revenue.

A spokesman said the problem was getting worse. "You can see why smokers buy them in these tough times when higher taxes make legal cigarettes more expensive," he said. "But this money goes to hardcore criminals involved in other activities such as drugs and people-trafficking. It's a problem across Europe and we need more government resources to fight it."

G

Britain 'cherry picking the benefits of Europe'

A top German politician last night savaged David Cameron's plans for Britain's referendum on EU membership.

Guido Westerwelle, Germany's foreign affairs minister, accused the UK of cherry-picking the benefits of the EU and he slammed any attempts to loosen ties with Brussels, claiming: 'We need more, not less Europe.'

He added: 'The European settlement may not be to everyone's liking, but that is the nature of every good compromise. There can be no cherry picking.

'Saying "You either do what I want or I'll leave" is not an attitude that works in personal relationships or in a community of nations.'

In pairs

Study the reports and then list them in order of what you both consider to be the importance of the issues they raise. For example, if you think D is the most important write down 1–D and so on.

In groups

Compare your lists. Talk about why you consider some issues to be more important than others.

Imagine your group is the editorial committee of a weekly TV news programme in which topical issues are discussed. Decide which four issues you would include in the programme. Then role play a discussion about one of the issues.

For your file

Choose one of the issues on which you have a strong opinion and write a letter expressing your views on the issue.

Cut out a newspaper report which raises an issue that you feel strongly about. Put it in your file and write a comment saying why you have chosen that particular report.

Separation and divorce

Dealing with divorce

Marie (14), Ellen (12) and Laura (10) have watched their parents get divorced. They talk about what they have learned from their experience.

Why do people get divorced?

Laura: Because they don't like each other as much as they did before.

Ellen: They are changing or have changed.

Marie: Each situation is unique and has its own set of reasons. Most reasons are too complicated and adult-related for parents to share with their children. That's OK. There are some things we really don't need to know. Don't be afraid to say that to a parent who is telling you things that you think are none of your business (but say it nicely!).

I'm scared about my parents' divorce. What can I do?

Laura: It's okay to be scared. I was scared when my parents got divorced. Just hang on in there!

Ellen: Your parents aren't spending as much time with you and they might be cranky. That doesn't mean they don't love you. They need some space and some time.

Marie: Of course you're scared – it's a scary thing. Think about why you are scared. Let your parents know what you are thinking.

They can reassure you. They're scared too, but you can all support each other.

Can I make my parents get back together?

Laura: No, and don't try. If they stay together, they won't be happy and they'll probably just fight.

Ellen: No. Lots of kids probably try, but it won't work, so don't get involved doing something that will just frustrate everyone.

Marie: Just like us, our parents have to choose their own paths. You can't do anything that will get them back together. It's their problem and their job to make life work for themselves. The decision to divorce is probably not something they made in a hurry. They've likely thought about all of the possibilities and they see this as the best thing to do.

Is it my fault that my parents are getting divorced?

Laura: No. How could it be? They're the grown-ups, you're just a kid.

Ellen: No. This is between your parents. There's nothing a kid could do that would cause a divorce.

In groups

Discuss what Marie, Ellen and Laura say about parents divorcing, and say whether or not you agree with them.

List all the different reasons you can think of why relationships between parents break up. Is it none of your business, or do you think children have a right to an explanation when their parents decide to split up? Does it depend on how old you are?

In groups

In groups, study each of the eight statements below. On your own, write down whether you agree with it (A), disagree with it (D) or are not sure (N/S). Then compare your views in a group discussion.

1 It's better for parents to split up than to stay together for their children's sake.

2 Splitting up is an easy option. Too many parents take the easy way out.

3 Children should never take one parent's side.

4 It's better for parents to split up than to spend all the time arguing and quarrelling.

5 Parents should involve children in discussions about splitting up.

6 A one-parent family can never be as happy as a two-parent family.

7 Parents who split up are selfish. They're only thinking of themselves.

8 Children are bound to suffer when parents split up.

A mixture of feelings

Young people often experience a mixture of feelings when their parents separate.

Whatever you feel, it's important to recognise your feelings and not to bottle them up. Talking can help. So find someone you can trust and talk to them openly.

Who decides who you live with?

In the majority of divorce cases, it's your parents who will decide which of them you are going to live with. They will also agree the arrangements for you to see your other parent. But if they are unable to agree, then the court will decide.

The court will take your views into consideration as well as those of your parents. The court may make two orders – a **residence order** and a **contact order**.

A residence order states which person you are going to live with. A contact order specifies the arrangements for you to see your absent parent. A typical arrangement is that you will spend alternate weekends with them and a week with them at Christmas, Easter and in the summer.

In pairs

'Children should always have the final say in deciding who they are going to live with.' Discuss this view.

Shock

"I just couldn't believe it. I felt totally numb. I went round in a kind of daze. It wasn't until my grandma talked to me that I realised I'd been suffering from shock."
– Nathan (14)

Anger

"I was furious with them both. I started taking it out on everybody and everything. I played truant from school and even got in trouble with the police. Of course, that just made things worse."
– Darrell (15)

Sadness

"I felt so unhappy. I just couldn't stop crying. We'd been such a happy family and now it was all over."
– Heather (13)

Guilt

"I got myself into a right state. I was convinced that I must be to blame."
– Alanna (14)

Relief

"To be honest, it was a relief. The tension had become so unbearable that I'd dread going home to find them fighting again. Now there was an end in sight."
– Mitchell (16)

Insecurity

"I felt frightened and insecure. I didn't know what was going to happen to me. Would we have enough money? Would I have to change schools? What would my friends think?"
– Kirsten (14)

For your file

Study Pat's letter (below) and write a reply.

My parents are separating and I feel it's all my fault. Whenever they argue it seems to be about me. Mum says Dad's too hard on me and he says I'm selfish and spoilt. I feel desperate. I'd do anything to help keep them together. I couldn't bear it if they split up. – Pat

Coping with change

If your parents separate there can be major changes in your life. You may have to move home or school. The parent you live with may be short of money. You may find it hard to keep contact with the absent parent. You may find it difficult if the parent you live with starts to form a new relationship.

In groups

Read the stories on this page and talk about the changes that these people had to face when their parents separated.

1 Talk about what it feels like to become part of a one-parent family after being in a two-parent family. How typical do you think Barbara's experience is?

2 Discuss Chris's problem and say what you think he should do about it.

3 Talk about what Xanthe says. Do you think her experience is unusual? Explain why.

A quarter of all teenagers whose parents divorce lose contact with the absent parent after 2 years. Discuss why you think this happens. How important do you think it is to try to keep in contact with both your parents after a divorce? Is it always desirable, whatever the circumstances? Give reasons for your views.

In pairs

Many children find it difficult to tell their friends and other people that their parents are separating. Discuss why they find it hard. Is it better to be upfront about it and to tell everybody, or do you think it's your family's business and that there's no need to tell anyone if you don't feel like it?

We had to move to a small flat

Barbara lived in a large house before her parents split up, but it has now been sold and Barbara is living in a small flat with her mother.

"It's not nearly as nice as our old place. She says it's only until she can get on her feet, and then we'll get a better place.

Also, she has to work full-time now. She's always tired – she comes in, does a few jobs around the flat and then collapses in front of the TV."

I want to be with my mates

Chris found that it was a problem pleasing both his father and himself. He felt really guilty because he was bored when he was with his dad.

"I spend every weekend with my dad. We really get on and I know he enjoys my visits. The trouble is, I end up feeling really bored. Dad makes me feel guilty because on a Saturday night I want to go out with my mates, not sit at home and watch TV, however much he likes having me around."

I get the best of both worlds

Some young people, like Xanthe, speak positively of an arrangement where they split their time between two parents.

"I actually enjoyed seeing my parents separately. We often used to find it difficult to agree on things, but now I do different things with my mum and with my dad. They make more of an effort to do things with me, like taking me ice-skating or to the cinema, and I make less of a fuss when they ask me to help out with chores and things like that. I feel I get the best of both worlds.

"I also spend more time with each of them on their own, and have got closer to them and know them better as people. Now that we have adjusted to life after the break-up, I actually prefer it like this to how it was before."

How to cope with **step-parents**

Living in a step-family

"I hated my step-mum, Sharon, but now I know her better, I think she's really sweet and nice. We disagree sometimes and she aggravates me a lot, but she's OK really." Janet (14)

"When I visited dad, it was fun having a step-brother to do things with, but my father wasn't there for me. He showed favouritism to my step-brother. He spent more time with him than me. I really felt pushed into the background."
Jason (16)

"I was gob-smacked when Mum told us she was pregnant. So were my step-brothers. We were pretty mean to Mum during her pregnancy. Amazingly when Pete was born it brought us together because he belonged to both families."
Rachel (16)

In groups

What do you learn from the statements above about the problems children have when settling in to a step-family? What other problems and difficulties might they face?

Study the article (right). Which do you think is the most useful piece of advice **a)** on how to cope with step-parents; **b)** on how to get on with step-brothers and step-sisters?

If you're going to be living with your step-parents, don't expect everything to be brilliant from the start. Everyone will have a lot of adjusting to do, and just getting used to each other's habits is a big step.

Your step-parent isn't a substitute for your real mum or dad. But that doesn't mean you can't form a close, loving relationship with him or her. Why not give it a chance?

If you do have problems with a step-parent, it can help to talk to someone who isn't closely involved, maybe a friend or a teacher you get on with. Often someone a bit more distant from the problem can stand back, take a good look and suggest things that might help.

Try to get to know your step-mum or dad as a person, don't just see them as a threat. Until you find out a bit about them and discover what their personality's like, how do you know you aren't going to get on?

If you really are having big problems with a step-parent, try having a private word with your mum or dad about it. They will want to sort things out.

Brothers and sisters

Adjusting to having a step-brother or step-sister also takes time. If you're having problems, think of the following:

All families are different. So if, for example, you're used to having a lie-in at weekends and your step-brothers and sisters like to get up at the crack of dawn and watch TV with the sound up high, you'll need to reach a compromise. Of course, that means talking about how you feel – not shouting!

If you do argue, it's not the end of the world. After all, regular brothers and sisters argue all the time, so it's only natural to argue with your new siblings, isn't it?

Try to see step-brothers and step-sisters as potential friends. If you each make an effort, you can end up close and good mates – much better than being at war with them!

Respect their space and privacy. Even if you have to share a room, work out a few ground rules between you so there aren't any misunderstandings.

Your mum or dad remarrying definitely takes a lot of getting used to and can be a very upsetting time. But if everyone makes the effort, you should end up as a happy family – it just takes a bit of effort and a lot of compromise all round.

For your file

A friend called Leah is very upset because her mother is getting remarried. She is feeling resentful and anxious about moving in with her step-father and his two children. She thinks she will have to share a bedroom. Write a letter offering Leah advice on how to cope with the new situation.

Safety at home

Every year thousands of people are injured in accidents at home. You should know what to do in an emergency.

+ First aid for fractures and breaks

1 If you think a bone is broken, do not move the person. This is particularly important if you think the neck or spine is injured because damage to the spinal cord can cause permanent paralysis.

2 Call an ambulance.

3 Keep the person warm.

4 Do not give the injured person anything to drink in case they need an anaesthetic later.

5 Do not move the casualty until you have immobilised the fracture, which means making sure it cannot move. Movement of the broken ends can cause more damage, pain and shock.

6 Immobilise a broken leg by putting some soft padding between the legs and tying the injured leg gently but firmly to the other leg at the ankles and knees. Immobilise a broken arm by putting the casualty's arm across the chest and supporting it with an arm sling.

+ First aid for burns and scalds

A burn or a scald damages your skin and destroys the blood vessels just below the surface. The first aid treatment is the same for burns and scalds.

1 Pour cold water over the burn at once. This reduces the heat in the skin. Keep putting on cold water for at least 10 minutes. Either hold the burn under a cold tap or dip it into a bowl or a bath of cold water.

2 Burnt skin often swells up. Take off anything near the burn that may be tight, such as jewellery or a watch.

3 Cover the burn with a clean dry dressing either from your first aid box or use a cotton pillow case or a linen tea towel. This will help to protect the skin from the risk of infection.

4 If the person is badly burned, call an ambulance.

5 Don't try to pull off any clothes that are stuck to the skin. Don't put any cream or ointment on the burn or use a fluffy cloth or cotton wool to cover the burn.

+ First aid for cuts

If someone loses too much blood their body won't get enough oxygen. Severe bleeding can cause death, so the first thing to do is stop the bleeding. Put your thumb and/or fingers on the wound and press firmly. For a large cut, try pressing the edges together. Keep pressing until the bleeding stops. This may take up to 15 minutes.

A large cut that has gaping edges may need stitches. For cuts with an object embedded, don't try to clean it or to take out any object from the wound. Removing it could cause more damage and might increase the bleeding, as the object may be plugging the wound. Bandage the wound with a clean dressing and get medical help.

If direct pressure won't stop the bleeding, press gently but firmly above and below the wound. If you can, raise the injured part so that it is above the level of the casualty's chest. This slows down the blood flow from the heart to the injured part.

If it is a small cut or a graze, clean the wound with soap and water, then dry it and put on a sterile dressing or an adhesive plaster. The size of the pad touching the wound must always be larger than the wound. Don't use any creams or ointments. They do not help and may delay healing by softening the skin.

In pairs

Discuss these questions, then write your answers.

1 Why is it dangerous if someone is bleeding badly? How would you try to stop the bleeding?

2 How would you treat:
a) a wound with an object embedded in it?
b) a grazed knee?

3 What first aid treatment would you give someone you suspect has:
a) a broken arm?
b) a broken leg?
c) a burn?

For your file

Find out what you should do if someone is suffocating or choking, then write first aid instructions: 'What to do if someone is suffocating' and 'What to do if someone is choking'.

Emergency first aid

When you are faced with an emergency, do not rush in immediately with first aid. Pause to assess the situation first. Look around to make sure that you are not going to endanger yourself or the casualty. You must then decide how the injury should be treated.

Unconsciousness

1 Check that the person is breathing properly. Make sure there are no obstructions in the mouth. Remove any false teeth, chewing gum or vomit.

2 Stop any severe bleeding by pressing firmly on the wound.

3 If the person stops breathing, give them mouth-to-mouth resuscitation immediately.

4 It can be dangerous for an unconscious person to lie on their back, because their tongue may fall back and block the airway. Once you are sure that breathing is

satisfactory and any severe bleeding is controlled you should put the person in the recovery position (see diagram). This prevents the tongue from falling back and allows any blood, fluid or vomit to drain out of the mouth.

5 It can be dangerous to move someone who has broken bones or has internal injuries. Do not move them unless you have to do so because of further danger, such as from traffic or fire.

6 Do not leave an unconscious person alone unless you have to because there is no one else around and you need to fetch help.

Shock

A person who has had a serious injury, severe pain or serious loss of blood may be suffering from the condition called shock. The symptoms of shock vary depending on the severity of the condition. The symptoms include paleness, feeling faint, cold and clammy skin, a weak and fast pulse, fast and shallow breathing. Shock can cause unconsciousness and even death. The aim of first aid for shock is to prevent the shock from getting worse.

1 Get the casualty to lie down and deal with any injuries.

2 If the casualty has lost a lot of blood, keep the head down and if possible raise the lower limbs. But do not do this if you think there may be a head injury or that a leg may be broken.

3 Cover the casualty with a blanket, rug or coat to keep him or her warm, but not too hot.

4 Do not give anything to drink in case the person needs to have an anaesthetic when they get to hospital.

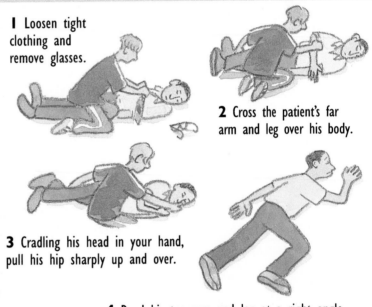

1 Loosen tight clothing and remove glasses.

2 Cross the patient's far arm and leg over his body.

3 Cradling his head in your hand, pull his hip sharply up and over.

4 Bend his top arm and leg at a right angle. Tilt his head back so that his chin juts forward.

In pairs

Draw up a list of 'Dos' and 'Don'ts' when giving emergency first aid to an unconscious person.

Discuss what shock is, what the symptoms are and how it should be treated.

Practise putting each other into the recovery position.

31

What is child abuse?

Child abuse is when adults hurt children or young people under 18, either physically or in some other way. Often the adult is someone the child or young person knows well, such as a parent, relative or friend of the family.

There are four main types of abuse:

Physical abuse includes hitting, kicking and punching, and may even lead to death.

Emotional abuse includes sarcasm, degrading punishments, threats and not giving love and affection, which can undermine a young person's confidence.

Neglect occurs when basic needs, such as food, warmth and medical care, are not met. Being thrown out of home may also be an example of neglect.

Sexual abuse occurs if an adult pressurises or forces a young person to take part in any kind of sexual activity. This can include kissing, touching the young person's genitals or breasts, intercourse or oral sex. If an adult asks you to touch his or her genitals, or to look at pornographic magazines or videos, these are examples of sexual abuse.

As well as causing suffering at the time, there may be long-term difficulties for young people who have been abused. All forms of abuse are wrong and have damaging effects on children and young people.

No one knows exactly why some adults take advantage of their position of authority over young people in this way. There may be many different reasons. Stress, unhappy circumstances, the feeling of having no power in adult relationships, and having been abused as a child may all play a part. But it is hard to predict with certainty which factors cause an adult to abuse a child.

Some adults may even convince themselves that there is nothing wrong with their behaviour, or that it is for the child's own good.

But whatever the reason, abuse is **always** wrong and it is **never** the young person's fault.

In groups

'A good hiding never did anyone any harm.'
Say why you agree or disagree with this view.

FACTS and FICTIONS about ABUSE

1 When a young person is abused, the offender is more likely to be a stranger.
FALSE – *In the majority of reported cases the offender is someone the young person knows.*

2 Girls are more at risk of abuse than boys.
FALSE – *Boys are at risk almost as much as girls, though boys report abuse less.*

3 The majority of offences of abuse are carried out by men.
TRUE – *Most reported cases of abuse are by men.*

4 Victims are sometimes to blame for the abuse because of the way they behaved.
FALSE – *It is never the victim's fault, no matter how they behaved. It is always the abuser's fault.*

5 If anyone attempts to touch you in a way that makes you feel uncomfortable, you have the right to tell them not to do so.
TRUE – *It is your body and you have the right to decide who touches you and who doesn't.*

Sexual abuse

I feel so guilty and ashamed

There was this friend of my dad's who I got on really well with. One evening he came round while my parents were out and put this video on which showed people having sex. He sat down beside me and put his arm round me and started touching me all over. I tried to tell him to stop but he wouldn't listen and made me touch him. He told me that what we were doing was all right and it was to be our secret. I've never told anyone about it before, because I feel so guilty and ashamed about what happened.

Kayleigh

If you are being abused, it is extremely important to understand that *you* haven't done anything wrong. The victim is *never* to blame for what happens to them, and yet so many victims of abuse feel guilty. No one deserves to be abused, and no matter how you react in a situation where you're being abused (whether you don't put up a fight, whether you maybe even experience sexual feelings that aren't entirely unpleasant) you are not responsible for what happened to you. If you have feelings of guilt, try to fight them, because you have *nothing* to feel guilty about. Concentrate instead on knowing that your abuser is in the wrong, and become determined to protect yourself and put things right.

The most important thing to do if you have been abused is to tell someone about it. Choose a responsible adult who you trust. If you're afraid to tell a parent or guardian (perhaps because the abuser is someone close to them), choose another older relative, a teacher you like or your doctor. If you can't think of anyone you'd feel comfortable talking to, or you think you might prefer to talk to someone you don't know, you can get help and advice by ringing a helpline.

NSPCC Child Protection Helpline: this is a free 24-hour service, which you can ring either if you think you are being abused yourself, or if you are worried about a friend. Telephone: 0808 800 5000.

Childline: this is a helpline for young people who are in trouble or danger. You can also contact them if you are concerned about a friend being abused. Telephone: 0800 1111.

What happens next?

When you tell an adult about serious abuse, they may have to involve other people to help you sort things out. Usually there will be a social worker, and sometimes a police officer and doctor.

What happens next is called an **investigation**. In order to help you, these professionals will ask you questions to find out exactly what happened. These questions may be embarrassing or difficult, but the adults involved are used to talking to young people who have had similar experiences, and should make it as easy as possible for you. As part of the investigation, the professionals will probably also speak to your family and other people who know you well. After the investigation there may be a **case conference** where the professionals will meet and make decisions about how best to help you. You might be able to go along to all or part of the case conference.

During the investigation and case conference, it is important that you make sure that the professionals know how *you* feel. Try not to be afraid to ask questions, and let them know how they could make things easier for you.

Young people who have been abused are only taken away from home if it is dangerous for them to stay. The majority stay in their own home. Most of those who are removed return home as soon as it is felt that they will be safe.

Saying no

If an adult starts pressurising you to do something you don't want to do, tell them firmly to stop.

With your partner, take it in turns to practise saying no. Role play a scene in which a friend is putting pressure on you to do something that is reckless or dangerous. Practise saying no politely but firmly.

Safety in the street

We would all like to be able to walk through the streets alone without feeling frightened, and we all have a right to be able to feel safe whatever we do.

Unfortunately, sometimes that is not always possible so it is important to know what we can do to make sure that we stay safe.

Staying safe in the street...

- Keep to main, well-lit paths.
- Don't walk closely behind people who are walking alone.
- Don't accept unorganised lifts.
- Invest in a personal alarm.
- Walk facing the traffic. Think about the clothes you are wearing if you have to walk home late at night. For example, trousers are more practical than tight skirts.
- If attacked shout FIRE – not 'rape' or 'help', as more people are likely to respond.
- Make sure that your mobile phone is charged.
- Be aware of your surroundings – especially at a cash point, telephone booth, near pubs and clubs.
- Tell someone where you are going and when you will be back.

Safety on buses...

- If you're waiting at a quiet bus stop at night, look to see if there's a café or shop that you can wait inside till your bus comes.
- At night don't go upstairs on a double-decker. Try to find an aisle seat and sit near the driver.
- Don't travel alone if you can avoid doing so.
- If you feel threatened, go and stand close to the driver and tell them why you are doing so.
- If you are getting off alone at a quiet stop, arrange for someone to meet you there.

❖ In groups

Discuss what you think a person should do in each of these situations.

1 You are travelling home on the bus late at night and a stranger comes and sits next to you and starts to chat you up.

2 You are walking along the street and a car pulls up alongside and the people inside offer you a lift.

3 You are travelling on a crowded bus and you feel someone stroking your thigh.

4 You are walking through a shopping precinct and you get the feeling that someone is following you.

5 You are walking past a group of people and they start shouting insults and making lewd comments.

6 You enter the hallway of the block of flats where you live and you see someone hanging about that you don't like the look of.

7 You are walking home with a friend who suggests that you take a short cut that will save you 20 minutes but it means going down a poorly-lit lane.

8 The person who said they'd drive you home has taken drugs or is drunk and you've no money to get yourself home.

Safety in public places

If you like to hang around in parks, on the beach, arcades, fast food places, shopping centres, or any other public place, take these precautions:

- Stay with your friends, or at least within sight of them.
- Avoid these places at night, especially if they are deserted or tend to attract gangs.
- Avoid deserted toilets.

Keep an eye out for a lone adult, especially a man or older boy, who hangs about where young people congregate. If he tries to make friends with you, or he offers you money, food, drink or drugs, refuse and act cold or distant. If he persists or you see him playing a lot with a particular child, tell your parents or another trusted adult nearby.

If someone talks to you persistently

'I was stuck on a train once during a breakdown, and this middle-aged man started chatting to me. I didn't like him because he was pushy, so I acted cold and moved away from him. He got the message, but then he turned to this other teenage girl and started talking to her. She was too embarrassed to be rude to him, and pretty soon he was touching her earrings and necklace and asking her about her boyfriends and making her blush. She looked embarrassed because everyone could hear.'

Don't let someone intimidate you into putting up with pushy, personal, or unpleasant conversation. If he's insensitive enough to keep bothering you, you don't have to worry about being rude to him. If brief, cold answers and a turned-away head don't stop him, pointedly moving away from him should. If you are absolutely stuck next to him in a rush-hour crowd, shout, 'There's a man bothering me here, please let me through.' Make sure he's the one who is embarrassed, not you.

The golden rule of self-defence

The golden rule of self-defence is to pay attention to, and trust your instincts. Countless victims of sexual assault and other crimes have said, 'I felt something was wrong, but I didn't want to look stupid, so I didn't do anything.' If you feel uncomfortable around a person or a place, if a warning signal goes off somewhere deep inside you, if you feel scared or just uneasy, don't ignore it. It is always better to act on your warning instincts and never know whether you were right than to ignore them and find yourself a victim; a moment of looking foolish is nothing compared to being assaulted.

In groups

Plan a short video for young people that tells them how to stay safe in the street. First, decide exactly what tips you want your video to give, then discuss how you are going to put your messages across. Draft a detailed plan for your video, then choose someone to explain it to the rest of the class and share your ideas in a class discussion.

For your file

Design a leaflet for young people called 'Safety in the street – how to protect yourself outside'.

Safety on the internet

Staying safe in chatrooms

When you are using a chatroom or posting on a message board, make sure that you never give out any personal information like your address or your phone number. You should always use a nickname, so no one can look you up in a telephone directory and get your home phone number.

It's usually not a good idea to meet someone that you've been chatting to online. Remember that you can never be sure that they are telling the truth about their age or their interests and you could be putting yourself in danger.

Remember:

- ☒ **Never** give out identifying information such as name, address, school name or telephone numbers in a public message such as a chatroom or a bulletin board.

- ☒ **Never** send anyone you don't know a picture of yourself.

- ☒ **Never** respond to messages or bulletin board items that are suggestive, threatening, obscene or generally make you feel uncomfortable.

- ☒ **Never** arrange a face to face meeting without telling your parent or guardian. If your parent or guardian agrees to the meeting, make sure you meet in a public place and have them with you.

- ☒ **Be careful** when someone offers you something for nothing, such as gifts or money. Be very careful about any offers that involve you going to a meeting or having someone come to your house.

- ☒ **Be sure** that you are dealing with someone that your parents know and trust before giving out any personal information about yourself via e-mail.

- ☒ **Remember** that people online may not be who they seem. Because you can't see or even hear the person it would be easy for someone to misrepresent himself or herself.

Keeping safe online:

Use the acronym **DANGER** to keep safe online:

Don't reply to messages that are threatening, suggestive or obscene.

Always use a nickname in chatrooms.

Never arrange a meeting without telling your parent or guardian.

Get an adult's advice before posting a picture on the internet.

Exchange personal information only with people you can trust

Remember that people online may not be who they say they are.

Role play

One of you says that you are going to arrange a meeting with someone you have been chatting to online. The other person tries to persuade you that it is not a good idea.

Self taken images – sexting

Someone taking an indecent image of themselves and sending it to their friend or boy/girlfriend by a mobile phone or some other form of technology is sometimes referred to as 'sexting'

Once these images have been taken and sent to others, control is lost of them and the images could end up anywhere. They could be seen by friends and family, a future employer, or even, in some cases, end up in the possession of an offender.

This also puts the person who sent the images in a vulnerable position, as somebody they may or may not know now has these images and could use technology to bully, harass or even locate them.

What can I do?

If you receive an indecent image or text from someone, do not send the image on to others. Report it to a responsible adult.

If you know that an indecent image of you or a friend has been posted on the online environment, you should contact the service provider, such as *Facebook* or *Youtube* to have it removed. You can do this by visiting their safety centres and following the reporting links.

The law

By sending indecent pictures of a person under 18 on to someone else you could be breaking the law.

If a teenager were to have in their possession an indecent image of another minor, they would technically be in possession of an indecent image of a child, which is an offence under the Protection of Children Act and the Criminal Justice Act.

Shop safely online

Follow these common sense rules to shop safely online.

- Make sure the company you are buying from uses a secure shopping server. You'll know it's a secure site if a padlock icon appears at the bottom of your browser window or the web address begins with 'https'.

- If you've never heard of the company before, search their site for any contact numbers and postal addresses. If they are a respectable company, they won't mind you giving them a quick call to ask them a few questions.

- Make sure that you never send your bank details to anyone in an e-mail. Legitimate banks and online stores will never ask you to do this as it is not a secure way of sending information.

- If you do receive an official-looking e-mail that asks you to send your financial details, you should never reply as you could become a victim of identity fraud.

Online rights and responsibilities

'I have the right to say whatever I like online. Stopping people from saying what they want and posting whatever pictures they want is censorship.'

'People have the responsibility not to say anything or post pictures of anything that other people find offensive.'

'The government should regulate the content of everything that is posted on line.'

'It's up to me to decide what sites I visit online. People have the right to access whatever they want.'

'All inappropriate and indecent material should be blocked.'

'It's all very well to say that certain material should be blocked, but who is to decide what is inappropriate and indecent?'

In groups

Discuss these statements and say why you agree or disagree with them.

For your file

Work with a partner and draft 'A responsible user's guide to social networking sites'.

Police duties and police powers

The duties of the police force are:

1 To protect life and property.

2 To maintain public order.

3 To prevent and detect crime.

The police often rely on help from the general public, and a lot of their information comes from what people tell them. To do their job, the police sometimes need to ask people questions and search their property. A lot of the law that sets out police duties and powers is contained in the Police and Criminal Evidence Act 1984.

Stopping

If a police officer stops you in the street, you are entitled to know the officer's name and the police station where they work. You are also entitled to know why the officer has stopped you. It is not acceptable for this to be because of your colour, dress, hairstyle or the fact that you might have been in trouble before.

You don't strictly have to answer an officer's questions, unless they suspect that you have committed (or are about to commit) an arrestable offence – such as theft, assault or carrying an offensive weapon. In these circumstances you must give your name and address, but need not answer any more questions.

REMEMBER If you're stopped by the police, keep calm and don't overreact. If you're obstructive and rude, you're more likely to be arrested. Staying calm will also help you remember what happened and what was said. Don't deliberately mislead the police by giving false information or wasting their time.

Searching

The police are allowed to search you for a number of reasons, but cannot do this by force unless you have been arrested or are suspected of carrying:

- drugs
- stolen goods
- weapons or anything that might be used as a weapon
- anything that might be used for burglary or theft.

If you are searched, the officer should explain why the search is taking place and what they expect to find.

Any search that involves more than a check of your outer clothing should be done out of public view or in a police station or van. If the search requires more than the removal of outer clothing, it should be done by someone of the same sex.

REMEMBER Stay calm, and make sure you know why you're being searched. If the police search you illegally, they are committing an assault, but if they have good reason, and you refuse, you may be charged with obstruction.

In groups

1 What did you learn from this page about powers the police have to "stop and search" you in the street?

2 Discuss the views on "stop and search" (right). Which do you agree with and why? Where appropriate, support your views by giving examples from your own experience.

"The police have too much power to interfere in our lives. The police powers of "stop and search" are an infringement of our liberty to move around freely."

"If the police didn't have the powers to "stop and search" people it would be even easier for criminals to break the law and get away with it."

Helping the police

If you are asked to go to a police station to help with enquiries, it's important to know whether you are being arrested. If you are being asked to go voluntarily, you may refuse (although the police may then decide to arrest you, and then you have to go).

If you are at the police station, you are entitled to send a message to your family or a friend telling them where you are, and also to free legal advice from a solicitor. If you have not been arrested, you may leave at any time you wish.

Questioning

If you are 16 or under you should never be interviewed without your parent or an appropriate adult (such as a teacher or social worker) being present. However, you should also have a solicitor present to advise you. You must give the police your name and address, but you have the right not to answer any further questions.

Reprimands, warnings and prosecutions

If you have broken the law, whether you will receive a reprimand or a warning or are prosecuted will depend on the offence, whether you admit it, and how many offences you have committed previously.

There are now limits on how many 'last chances' the police can give you before you end up in court. If you commit a really serious offence you will be prosecuted straight away. If you commit a less serious offence, the police can give you a maximum of only two chances before you will definitely be taken to court.

As soon as you break the law, even for something you might consider minor (like dropping litter or riding a bicycle on the pavement), the police will give you a reprimand for the first time and a warning for the second time. If you break the law for a third time you will automatically be sent to court and prosecuted.

If you are given a reprimand, the police officer will talk to you about what you have done and explain what will happen if you break the law again. They will remind you about who you have hurt by breaking the law – your family as well as your victim. The police will keep a record of your crime. You may find that your details are passed on to a Youth Offending Team who will decide if any further action should be taken.

If you are given a warning, the police will talk to you and put your crimes on record in the same way as for a reprimand. You are automatically referred to a Youth Offending Team who will generally decide what type of scheme to put you on to stop you committing any more crimes.

Reprimands and warnings can only be given to people who have admitted that they have broken the law. This means that someone who has committed an offence and does not admit it cannot be given a reprimand or warning. In these cases they will be sent to court and prosecuted.

Prosecution means your case will be heard in the Youth Court. If you are found guilty, you will be sentenced, and will have a criminal conviction.

What records are kept on young offenders?

A record of your final warning will be kept by the police and the Youth Offending Team until you are 18 years old. If you offend again, this will help them to decide if any further action should be taken. A reprimand or final warning is not a conviction and does not constitute a criminal record.

If you are 10 or 11 years old, the records on you will stay 'live' on the Police National Computer until your 17th birthday. If you are older, the records will stay active for five years.

In groups

Discuss what you learn from this page about the system for dealing with young people who break the law. Do you think it is fair always to prosecute a person for their third offence, however minor their first two offences might have been? Give reasons for your views.

Keeping the peace

A lot of police time is spent controlling large crowds. As well as looking after crowds at football matches and other sporting events, the police also supervise demonstrations and public protest meetings. Every year the Metropolitan Police deals with several hundred demonstrations and processions in central London.

The police attend demonstrations and disputes to make sure that the law is not broken, and to protect both sides. Many demonstrations are carried out peacefully and no incidents occur. Occasionally, though, violence breaks out and the police have to act to protect people and property.

Sometimes the police are accused of causing trouble by the way they treat demonstrators. From reports you have read in the newspapers or seen on television, do you think there is any evidence that the police cause trouble at demonstrations?

"The police might have been on duty at a demonstration for hours. Then you have just one flare-up as one small group gets out of hand. A few helmets roll in a scuffle, and a couple of demonstrators get dragged to a police van. It makes good television, just right for the introduction to the news bulletin, but it gives a totally false picture of what has been going on. We know for a fact that television cameras and their spotlights egg a crowd on." – Senior police officer

In groups

Discuss times when you have been in a large crowd that the police have been controlling. Talk about the way the police handled the crowd and any incidents that occurred. What do you think of the way the police controlled the crowd?

Discuss what the senior police officer said. Do you think television often presents a distorted picture of what happens at demonstrations?

Keeping you safe

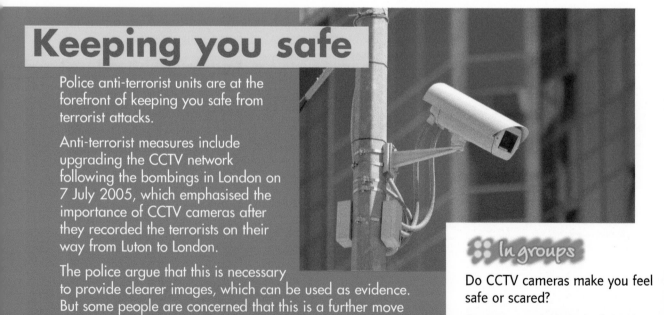

Police anti-terrorist units are at the forefront of keeping you safe from terrorist attacks.

Anti-terrorist measures include upgrading the CCTV network following the bombings in London on 7 July 2005, which emphasised the importance of CCTV cameras after they recorded the terrorists on their way from Luton to London.

The police argue that this is necessary to provide clearer images, which can be used as evidence. But some people are concerned that this is a further move towards a 'surveillance society' with cameras following your every move.

In groups

Do CCTV cameras make you feel safe or scared?

Are you worried about living in a surveillance society?

What do you think of the police?

In groups

What is your attitude towards the police? On your own, study each of the statements (below) and decide whether you agree with it, disagree with it or are not sure. Then share your views in a class discussion.

1 People don't respect the police as much as they should.

2 You can rely on the police to help you if you are in trouble.

3 The police are friendly and polite.

4 The police are good at catching criminals and maintaining law and order.

5 The police are racist and treat white people better than black or Asian people.

6 The police have a difficult job and they do it as well as they can.

7 The police are bullies and misuse their authority.

8 Teenagers don't like the police because the police don't like teenagers.

9 The police interfere in our lives too much.

10 The media only report the mistakes the police make, not all the good things they do.

For your file

Write a short statement saying what you think of the way the police behave and what your attitude to the police is.

Doing a good job?

Some people see the police as a nuisance, or even as the enemy, but others think they are just doing a job that can save lives and make our society a better place.

A survey of 270 people who took part in the rioting in British cities in August 2011 found that 85% thought that policing was a key factor in why the riots happened.

The most common complaints were related to stop and search and the basic incivility police were accused of displaying in everyday interactions with communities.

One 17-year-old Muslim boy told of being stopped by police on his way to school when he was 13. "One of them said to the other: 'Mate, why don't you ask him where Saddam is. He might be able to help.' They're supposed to be law enforcement. I hate the police."

73% of those surveyed had been stopped and searched by the police in the past year. They felt the police treated them like criminals regardless of what they had or hadn't done.

"Young people cannot walk down the street without the police stopping them,' said a 27-year-old woman from Salford. [They say] 'Take your hat off, take your hood off, empty your pockets, there's four of you, you've got to split up, you can't go round in a group' – even when you are not doing anything wrong."

Asked 'Do the police in your area do a good or bad job?', only 7% said 'excellent' or 'good' compared with 56% of those who took part in the British Crime survey.

In groups

"The police in our area do a good job"

Explain why you agree or disagree with this statement.

Gambling – the lure and the law

Gambling is a popular leisure activity. The nature of gambling has changed in recent years. The National lottery and online gambling have replaced football pools, bingo and horse-racing as the most popular forms of gambling.

You are not allowed to buy a lottery ticket until you are 18. However, surveys suggest that 90% of under 18s have gambled at least once.

Why do young people gamble?

"It's glamorous. You see people in films and on TV gambling and you want to be like them."

"It's fun. It gives you something to do when you're bored."

"It's exciting. You're taking a risk and it gives you a real buzz waiting to see if you've won."

"It's a way of escaping from the real world and all your problems."

"The people I know who gamble do it because they can't stop themselves. They're addicted."

"People gamble to try and win lots of money to make their dreams come true."

A fixed-odds betting terminal in a casino

Winners and losers

Very few people who gamble win huge amounts of money. Most people lose the money they gamble. The odds are stacked against you. For example, there's a 14 million to 1 chance of winning the jackpot in the National Lottery, and a 35 to 1 chance of winning at roulette.

The winners are the betting shops and casino owners. The gambling industry is big business, generating a profit of £5.6 billion a year.

The other big winner is the UK government, which receives £1.7 billion a year in taxes on gambling.

For your file

Write a statement saying what you think are the reasons why people gamble.
Find out all you can about fixed odds betting terminals (FOBTs). Does what you discover support the view that FOBTs are the cause of an increase in the number of gambling addicts? Give reasons for your view.

Gambling – What do you think?

"Gambling can become an addiction, which ruins people's lives. It's wrong to call it harmless fun."

"People who condemn gambling are killjoys."

"It's like drinking alcohol – all right in moderation."

"I've never bought a lottery ticket. I don't see the point of gambling."

Discuss these views. What is your attitude to gambling?

Why is gambling condemned in some religions? Make a list of all the moral and religious arguments against gambling you can think of and say why you agree or disagree with them.

There are plans to build a supercasino in your area. Would you be for or against it? Explain why.

The National Lottery

Since its introduction in November 1994, the National Lottery has proved a huge success. Around 70% of adults play on a regular basis.

The success of the National Lottery means that by July 2008 £22 billion had been distributed to 'good causes', such as sports and arts projects, funded by the National Lotteries charities board. The National Lottery contributed almost £2.2 billion towards the funding for the London 2012 Olympic Games and Paralympic Games.

However, many charities reported that there was a significant fall in the amount of donations they received after the introduction of the lottery. Critics also argue that it is wrong for the lottery to be run as a profit-making venture and that the licence to run the lottery in future should go to a non-profit-making organisation. They also say that the introduction of the lottery has led to the creation of a gambling culture, in which more people are interested in and addicted to gambling. In particular, it encourages lots of the poorest members of society to spend money they cannot afford on lottery tickets rather than essentials, such as food and clothing.

4.5p Running costs
0.5p Camelot
12p Government
50p Prizes
28p Good causes
5p Retailers

Where each pound spent on a lottery ticket goes

In groups

Talk about the National Lottery. What do you think of the criticisms that are made about the way it is run and the influence that it has had? Do you think introducing the National Lottery was a good idea? Do you think any changes should be made to the National Lottery? Give reasons for your views.

Problem gambling

'Gambling has taken over my life!'

Two young people talk about how gambling has affected their lives.

Keri

Keri is 14 and spends all her money on scratchcards

66 The first time I bought a scratchcard I felt nervous. But all my friends were doing it and I didn't want to be left out. I didn't win but one of my friends did and I couldn't wait to have another go.

I went back next day and won a tenner. It gave me such a great feeling. When I won again the next week I began to think I was one of those people who was born lucky. Especially as none of my friends were winning.

They began to lose interest and started saying it was a mug's game. But it's got so I don't think I could live without doing them. 99

Jason

Jason is 15 and addicted to arcade machines

66 I started playing the machines when I was 12. I found it really exciting, especially the noise and flashing lights when I won. Before I knew it I was hooked. I couldn't wait to get down the arcade.

I spent all my money and savings, so I sold things from home to get cash. I even stole my sister's mp3 player. The breaking point came when I got caught shoplifting.

I now go to a counsellor who's really helpful. But it's been hard stopping, especially as some of my mates keep asking me to go down the arcade with them. 99

In groups

Discuss the effect that gambling has had on Jason and Keri's lives.

Role play

Role play the following scenes:

1 A group of friends are discussing what to do. Two of them want to go to an amusement arcade to play the machines and try to put pressure on the other two to go with them. Take it in turns to be the two who don't want to go, and discuss ways of saying no firmly.

2 A gang of friends are planning to pool their money to buy some scratchcards and to share any winnings. One of the friends is against the idea and thinks they'd get more value for money if they went to the swimming pool or the fairground instead. Take it in turns to be the 'odd one out'.

Facebook Accused of Creating Gambling Addicts

Facebook has been accused of turning 13–17 year olds into gambling addicts through the Las Vegas-style casino games available on its site.

Children are using 'virtual coins' to simulate the thrill of hitting the jackpot with slot machine and roulette games on their home computers and mobile phones.

There are now hundreds of virtual slot machines and poker games on Facebook, including *Jackpotjoy*, *Slotomania* and *DoubleDown Casino*.

But addiction experts have warned that the games encourage teenagers to think gambling is harmless fun.

From *Mail Online* 15 July 2012

For your file

Write an article for a magazine for young people about teenage gambling, describing the problems that it can cause and offering advice on how to gamble responsibly.

Wherever you are, when you watch football on TV you can bet on anything from 'next score' to 'dog on the pitch'. You have the chance to place hundreds of bets per match. But will it turn us all into gambling addicts?

No. Having a small bet on a football match increases the fun.

Yes. One bet leads to another and before you know it you've lost all your money. So you try to win it back next game and before you know it you've got a problem cause you're in debt.

In groups

What's your view of betting during football matches? Can it lead to a gambling problem?

"Internet gambling must be policed to stop young people gambling on it."

"All new computers should have a built-in device to stop pop-ups that advertise gambling."

"Gambling creates more misery and hardship than it gives pleasure."

Do you agree or disagree with these views? Explain why.

Until 2007 adverts for casinos, betting shops and online gambling sites were banned. What are the arguments for and against reintroducing the ban?

Making friends

Discuss the list of statements about friends and friendships. Decide whether you think each statement is **a)** true, **b)** sometimes true, **c)** not true. Make a note of your views, then join up with another pair and share your views in a group discussion.

The secret of making friends

Anita Naik offers advice on how to make and keep friends

Be patient and sensitive

No matter how much you like someone, don't demand too much, too soon; it may freak the other person out. No one likes to be pushed into things, nor to feel suffocated by another's attentions. Chill out, and let the relationship grow naturally.

Listen to your own conscience

If a prospective friend does something that makes you feel uncomfortable, don't be afraid to break off. Likewise, if someone makes you feel bad about yourself, then dump them – they're no good for you. So that bad feelings aren't left to ferment and therefore cloud whatever remains of the friendship, be up-front and let them know what's bugging you.

Learn to be trusting

It's impossible to have a friendship if there is no trust. Both people have to be open, honest and not afraid to say no.

Be forgiving

Some people just can't cut it in the friendship stakes; they may let you down, stand you up, or blab something that was meant to be just between the two of you. What you've got to do is understand the limits of particular friendships.

You must not think that one disappointing friendship means that they'll all be disappointing. Learn to understand and forgive your friends their shortcomings. There will be some people who will always be there for you, and there will be others who won't.

It's okay to have lots of friends

Without being at all disloyal, you can have different friends for different things. Some mates are sports team buddies, others are school pals and others you see only once a week at dance class. To some friends you will be an open book and they will know all your deepest, darkest fears. Other friends will only know the barest details. That's fine. Don't get worked up about making every friend a best friend.

The rules of friendship

1 Keep your friends' secrets.
2 Wait for your friend to offer secrets: do not pry.
3 Share your happy times as well as your sad times.
4 Stand up for your friends.
5 Show loving support.
6 Ask your friends for support when you need help.
7 Offer help: do not just wait for your friend to ask.
8 Make sure you return borrowed things.
9 If your friend hurts your feelings, say so. Don't go off in a sulk.
10 Look in your friend's eyes when you talk.
11 Don't joke about or tease your friend.
12 Don't be jealous of your friend's other relationships.

For your file

Write your views on friends and friendships. Say how important friendships are to you, what you value most in a friendship and what your expectations of friendships are.

Discuss what Anita Naik says about how to make and keep friends.

Make lists of **a)** the types of behaviour that help to cement a friendship, **b)** the kinds of behaviour that are likely to destroy a friendship.

Problems with friendships

Growing ← → Apart

"Quite frankly, I now find him boring a lot of the time I'm with him. But when he doesn't come round like he used to, then I miss him."

Mike

Most friendships start because the two people involved have lots in common, so when one of you grows up faster than the other and one of you finds new interests it can change everything between you. If that happens, it's sad; but often the only thing to do is to have a bit of a break from being best friends and each see other friends who share your interests.

If you and your friends are growing apart …

Don't

✗ make the situation into a big row so you end up falling out forever and making yourself even more unhappy. OK, so you don't have much in common with each other just now — but maybe in a few months you'll find one or both of you has changed and you might just want to be mates again! Give each other a bit of space, but try to keep in touch.

✗ blame yourself. This hasn't happened because you're a terrible friend or there's something wrong with you — it's simply that people change.

✗ feel bad if you're the one who feels you're growing out of your old mates. It's not like you're doing it on purpose and it happens to lots of people — it's all part of growing up.

Do

✓ see this as an opportunity to make new mates rather than fretting too much about the past. If you're the one who's feeling dumped it's easy to wallow in self-pity and lose your confidence, but look at it this way — now you're free to find mates who you really have things in common with.

✓ remember that you won't be the only one going through this. It's easy to imagine everyone else has lots of friends already and won't want you, but if you look closer you'll probably see other mates are going through sticky patches over exactly the same kind of problems.

✓ confide in someone at home about what's going on so you can get a bit of extra support while you're making some new friends.

What is a friend?

1. A friend must share your interests.
2. A friend is someone you can trust.
3. A friend should have a similar personality to you.
4. A friend should share your values.
5. A friend should always cover up for you.
6. A friend is someone who you can tell your private thoughts and feelings.
7. A friend is someone who won't tease you.
8. A friend must be approved of by your parents.
9. A friend is someone who won't disagree with you.
10. A friend is someone who will forgive you.

In groups

Study 'What is a friend?'. Discuss whether you agree or disagree with each rule. Are there any others you would add to the list? Are there any you would take off? Which three rules do you think are the most important?

Study the article on growing apart. Discuss the advice on how to deal with the situation of friends growing apart.

How much are you influenced by your friends?

How do you behave when you're with your friends? Do you let your friends influence your decisions, or do you always make up your own mind and do what you think is right? Do this quiz to find out how much you let your friends influence you. Keep a record, and then check what your answers tell you about your behaviour when you are with your friends.

1 **Your friend says something you do not agree with.** *Do you…*

a agree with them to avoid an argument?

b only say what you think if they ask your opinion?

c tell them you don't agree with them and explain why?

2 **Some friends dare you to do something reckless that could have serious consequences.** *Do you…*

a agree to do it in order to try to impress them?

b find an excuse for not doing it?

c refuse and say you're not prepared to be so reckless?

3 **A group of your friends are teasing someone and making hurtful remarks about them.** *Do you…*

a join in because they expect you to do so?

b not join in, but do nothing to stop them?

c try to get them to stop?

4 **You have become friends with someone none of the rest of your friends like.** *Do you…*

a drop your new friend?

b ask your friends their reasons then decide what to do?

c tell them that it's none of their business and you'll be friends with who you choose?

5 **Your friends ask you to do something that may get you into trouble with the police.** *Do you…*

a join in because everyone else is?

b try and persuade them it's wrong, but go along with them if they won't listen?

c tell them you're not joining in and walk away?

6 **Two of your friends have a row and fall out.** *Do you…*

a take the side of the person you like best?

b leave them to sort it out and try not to get involved?

c listen to both sides and support whoever you think is in the right?

7 **One of your friends asks you to lie to stop them getting into trouble with their parents.** *Do you…*

a agree to do so because you are afraid of losing their friendship?

b say you'll only do so if you are not covering up anything serious?

c say no and explain that you can't get involved in what's going on between them and their parents?

8 **Your friends are talking about sex in a way that you don't like.** *Do you…*

a join in, even though you feel uncomfortable?

b keep quiet, but not show your disapproval?

c tell them why you don't like the way they are talking?

What do your answers tell you about how much you are influenced by your friends?

Mostly 'a's You are so concerned about what your friends think of you that you will do almost anything to keep in with them. You're allowing them to influence you so much that you've stopped thinking for yourself. You need to listen far more to what your instincts and conscience tell you about how to behave than to think about what will most impress your friends. You must start asserting yourself and acting according to your beliefs rather than just doing things to please others.

Mostly 'b's You hesitate before saying or doing things that you don't believe in, and sometimes you allow yourself to do things that you don't want to do in order not to upset your friends. When faced with an awkward situation you tend to look for the easy way out. You need to start trusting your own judgement more and to be more prepared to speak out and do things that might set you apart from the crowd.

Mostly 'c's You have a healthy disregard for what others might think of you and are prepared to stand up for yourself and do what you believe is right. Sometimes it will cause difficulties with friends, but you understand that it is more important to stick to your principles rather than to do things just to curry favour. Your actions give you self-respect because you don't allow people to pressurise you, and those people who are your friends know where they stand with you and can rely on you to speak your mind.

In pairs

Talk about what you have learned from this activity about how much influence you let your friends have on you.

Gangs – know the facts

- A gang is not simply a group of friends who hang around together. Gangs intimidate people.

- Gangs rule by fear, and this doesn't just apply to the people they pick on. Often, gang members get involved in trouble because they're too afraid to back out, in case they look soft. Peer pressure is very common in gangs.

- Although you may not be doing anything illegal, if you're part of a gang, you're more likely to attract the attention of the police. Young people's characters are often judged by who they mix with; if you hang around with a wild lot, outsiders will assume you're the same.

- If you are being picked on by a gang, tell your parents, teacher or any other adult in authority. It's difficult to stand up to bullies when they are part of a group and you're on your own – that's why you need adult help. Don't be afraid to ask for it.

In groups

Study the article 'Gangs – know the facts' (left). Why do people go round in gangs? Discuss the way people behave in gangs. Talk about your experiences of gangs and say what you think of the way gangs treat their members and people who aren't members.

Gangs

"*I used to be part of a gang. But they made me do things I didn't want to do and I got into trouble. Now I steer clear of them.*"

"*Belonging to a gang is great. You really feel you're somebody. We do all kinds of crazy things together. It's a great laugh.*"

"*I think people who go round in gangs are weak. They give each other courage to do things they're too cowardly to do on their own.*"

For your file

Write a story about someone who allows a friend to pressurise them into doing something which they later regret.

The influence of advertising

Everywhere you go there are advertisements. Advertisers know that the more visible their product is, the more likely you are to buy it. So they are willing to spend large sums of money to promote their goods or services. An advert that interrupts the programme you are watching at peak time on TV may last for less than a minute, but the advertiser is willing to pay the TV company hundreds of thousands of pounds to broadcast it.

The money that advertisers pay to media institutions, such as TV companies, newspapers and magazines, provides them with most of their revenue. Without the money from advertising, the programmes broadcast by independent radio stations and commercial TV companies would not get made, and most of the magazines and newspapers you read would not get published.

Is advertising good or bad?

Some people would argue that it is wrong to use advertising to persuade people to buy things, especially things they might not really need. They also think that many advertisements are not strictly truthful when they claim that this washing powder is new and improved, or that cats love this particular brand of cat food.

The other side of the argument is that without advertising people would be less aware of what was available for them to buy. Also, that if manufacturers compete with one another to produce goods then they must compete to sell them as well.

How much influence do adverts have on you?

Some people argue that adverts have less influence than is often made out. They say that most people are suspicious of the claims that advertisers make. They suggest that the most popular TV ads are enjoyed because they are entertaining and funny, rather than because they are informative about the product, and that they don't really influence people to buy the product.

However, there is plenty of evidence to suggest that advertising does work. Retailers are often informed before a TV advertising campaign is about to take place in their area, so that they can stock up on the product in advance, and be in a position to meet the demand for the product that a campaign is likely to generate. Successful campaigns do lead to increased sales.

In groups

How much do you think you are influenced by advertisements? Talk about your favourite TV ads and why you like them. Are they for products that you are likely to go out and buy? If so, do you think the adverts have made you more likely to go out and buy them?

Discuss the views below. Say why you think advertising is either a good thing or a bad thing.

"Advertising encourages people to be materialistic and to want things they don't really need."

"There's nothing wrong with advertising. It keeps people informed and encourages competition, which benefits everybody."

Advertising and children

In the UK the Advertising Standards Authority regulates the content of advertisements and there are special rules for advertisers who target children under 16.

- Adverts cannot encourage children to have an unhealthy lifestyle. Junk food adverts are banned during TV programmes aimed at under 16s.
- Adverts must not take advantage of the natural sense of credulity and loyalty of children.
- Advertisers cannot suggest that not having a product will make a child inferior or that having the product will make the child more popular.
- Advertisements must not put pressure on a child to buy a product or to ask their parents to buy it.

The UK rules are some of the toughest in Europe. But they are not as strong as in Sweden where television adverts aimed at children under 12 are banned. Swedish law also bans displays of sweets within reach of young children and says that shops must pay attention to problems that could occur when parents are queuing up.

Shock tactics

Some advertisements use shock tactics. Public service adverts to discourage the use of drugs may show images of people covered in sores living in squalor, while road safety adverts may show a drunken driver knocking down a child. Charities trying to raise money to reduce world hunger and poverty may show distressing pictures of sick children.

In groups

Discuss these views:

"What bothers me about advertising is that they stereotype people."

"Many adverts are sexist."

"Adverts shouldn't show dying or badly injured people."

"There's too much fuss about what adverts contain. Advertisers should be free to include whatever they think is appropriate."

"The Chinese government is right. Adverts for expensive goods create a materialistic society."

What is the most shocking advertisement you have seen?
What do you think of advertisements that use shock tactics?

China bans adverts for extravagance

The Chinese government has banned TV and radio adverts that promote expensive gifts as part of its campaign against corruption and excess.

China's media watchdog said that encouraging viewers to splash out on watches or gold helped spread 'incorrect values and a bad social ethos.'

Daily Telegraph, 7 February 2013

In groups

Do you think there should be a total ban on TV adverts aimed at children?

Should any ban apply only to particular items? In Greece, for example, there is a ban on advertisements for children's toys between 7am and 10pm and a total ban on advertisements for war toys. Discuss your views and give your reasons.

What bothers you about adverts?

A survey of 11–16-year-olds found that they were most bothered by adverts which they found to be "too sexy".

They were also upset when people died or were hurt, when an advert was too scary or was unfair and nasty about certain types of people.

The main reasons they gave were:

- 10% were concerned that an advert was unfair or nasty about certain types of people,
- 11% found an advert too scary,
- 15% were upset because people died or were hurt
- 25% were bothered because an advert was too sexy.

For your file

**Use the internet to find out about 'advergames'.
Do you think they should be banned? Write a paragraph expressing your views.**

The commercial break

The most important feature of any advertisement is suggestion. Advertisements work by suggesting, for example, that if you buy their product you'll be happier or healthier, you'll improve your appearance, you'll have a cleaner home or have a faster, more efficient car.

Advertisements prey on your fears too. For example, take clothing ads. Many of them work by suggesting that it's cool to wear a particular brand and you need to wear that brand in order to fit in. The message is – if you don't wear it you're out of touch with fashion.

Advertisers use celebrities to endorse their products. The advertiser thinks that if you like the person you'll believe what they say or because you admire the person you'll use the product in order to be like them.

Mini-movies

When TV advertising began, most advertisements focussed clearly on the product and on giving information as to why you should buy it. Many of today's commercials are mini-movies – short clips of video with a plotline and the product is only mentioned at the end. Advertisers want you to remember the product by associating it with what happens in the plot.

Words and music

Advertisers pick their words and music to be memorable. For example, they choose short snappy slogans like the Macdonald's 'I'm Lovin' It'. Sometimes, the slogan is humorous and based on a pun, such as 'Do me a Quaver' (the Quavers snack slogan), or 'Brilliant cleaning begins with a Finish' (for Finish dishwasher powder).

Some advertisements use well-known songs so that the song and the product become linked. Others use jingles – short catchy rhymes that are easy to pick up, sing along with or remember after only one or two hearings.

In groups

Discuss what you learn from the article 'The commercial break' and draw up a list of the various techniques that are used in TV advertisements. Talk about recent TV ads and discuss which of these techniques they use.

Imagine you were in charge of planning a TV advertising campaign for a new product aimed at young people of your age, for example, a new bicycle model. Discuss your ideas for a 30-second advert and prepare a proposal to present to the rest of the class.

Plan and produce a radio advert for a new product. Discuss how many radio adverts include a catchy piece of music with simple lyrics called a jingle. Draft your script, choose appropriate music and compose a jingle to advertise your product. Then make a recording of your advert and play it to the rest of the class.

For your file

Find an advert in a newspaper or magazine and write an analysis of it. Comment on what its message is, who it is aimed at and how the words and pictures are used to create an image of the product that will encourage the target audience to want to buy it.

Sponsorship

Another way companies use the power of the media to get their message across is through **sponsorship**. One form of sponsorship involves paying for the right to have their name associated with a particular event. An example of this is when a company sponsors a sporting event so that the advertiser's name forms part of the event's title. In the 2013–14 seasons, English football teams played each other in the Barclays Premier League and the Sky Bet Championship. Every time the event is reported in the press, on the radio or TV, the sponsor gets a mention.

Another form of sponsorship involves paying teams or individuals to wear names and logos printed on their clothes. Sporting celebrities sponsored by sportswear companies include tennis player Andy Murray sponsored by Adidas and golfer Rory McIlroy sponsored by Nike.

Andy Murray has a £15 million 5 year deal with Adidas

Celebrityendorsement

Advertisers use celebrities to promote their products because it helps them to make their brands stand out. Using a celebrity helps what is known as the 'recognition factor'.

It also increases the chances of getting press coverage. Every time their celebrity gets their face in a newspaper or magazine it increases the possibility of them being associated with the product they are endorsing.

In groups

Would you buy something just because a famous person plugged it? According to some, it depends on the star and the product. Discuss this view.

Study this list of celebrities: Beyoncé Knowles-Carter, David Beckham, Carol Vordeman, Will.i.am, Paris Hilton, Lewis Hamilton, Victoria Beckham, Rory McIlroy, Jamie Oliver, Lady Gaga. Discuss which of these celebrities are most likely to influence you to buy the product or service that they are endorsing? Which are the least likely?

Are you making the most of your leisure time?

A test-yourself quiz

Do this quiz to find out about how well you spend your leisure time. Keep a record of your answers, and then check what your answers tell you about what use you make of your leisure time.

1 At the weekend, do you:
a Always plan in advance what you are going to do?
b Sometimes plan things in advance?
c Never plan ahead – just wait to see what happens?

2 How much time do you spend each week on your hobby?
a 4–6 hours.
b 1–3 hours.
c Less than an hour.

3 What types of TV programmes do you mainly watch?
a 'Serious' programmes, such as documentaries, news and drama.
b A mixture of serious programmes and light entertainment.
c Light entertainment, such as comedies, soaps, pop music and quizzes.

4 How often do you stay after school for a club or a practice?
a Two or three times a week.
b Once a week.
c Hardly ever.

5 When you go out with your friends do you usually:
a Go somewhere to do something, for example, go to a film or a disco, or to a park to play football?
b Go shopping or to a café?
c Hang about hoping someone might suggest something to do?

6 How often do you read a book other than a schoolbook?
a Most days.
b Every now and then.
c Hardly ever.

7 How often do you exercise (apart from in PE lessons)?
a 5–6 days a week.
b 2–3 days a week.
c Hardly ever.

8 When you go on a computer, what do you mostly use it for?
a Finding information on the internet.
b Visiting social networking sites.
c Playing games.

9 How do you keep up with what's going on in the world?
a By watching the news/reading a newspaper daily.
b By watching the news every now and then.
c By relying on other people to tell you if something happens.

10 If you are asked to volunteer to take part in a community activity do you usually:

a Volunteer?

b Wait to see if your friends volunteer?

c Never volunteer?

11 How often in the holidays do you feel bored because you can't think of anything to do?

a Very rarely.

b Sometimes.

c Most days.

12 How much time each day do you spend watching TV?

a Less than 1 hour.

b Between 1 and 3 hours.

c Over 3 hours.

What do your answers say about how you spend your leisure time?

Mostly 'a's You make very good use of your leisure time. You have plenty of interests and hobbies and you plan activities to do at the weekend and with your friends. You are prepared to volunteer for things and are involved in after-school activities. You look after yourself too by taking plenty of exercise. So you shouldn't get bored. But make sure you don't wear yourself out with all your activities. Allow yourself some time just to relax!

Mostly 'b's Your attitude to your leisure time is the same as many people's. Sometimes you plan ahead and you get actively involved in the things you like doing on a fairly regular basis. You've got a more relaxed attitude to life than the people who get mostly 'a's. But you could be making better use of your leisure time than you are. If you want to achieve more in your leisure pursuits, you'll need to put your mind to doing so.

Mostly 'c's You're not getting as much out of your leisure time as you could be. If your life seems boring much of the time, then you need to ask yourself why. Things won't change unless you do something to make them. Otherwise you'll continue to drift through life getting less out of it than you could be.

In pairs

Talk about what you have learned from this activity. How well do you use your leisure time and how good are you at the following:

■ Planning how you spend your time.

■ Getting involved in activities at school and in the community.

■ Using your leisure time to develop your knowledge and skills.

Each decide on one or more things you could do to make better use of your leisure time.

I never have any time to myself

"My problem is I hardly get any time to myself. By the time I've done my chores and then my homework, I'm exhausted. All I want to do is watch TV or listen to my DVDs. And at the weekend I never have any time to myself because I'm expected to do things with the family. What can I do? It's really getting me down." – Peta

Four Ways to Make Better Use of Your Leisure Time

1 Ration how much TV you watch.

2 Stay at school once a week for an after-school club.

3 Go out for a jog or a bike ride every other day.

4 Spend at least 20 minutes a day reading a book, magazine or newspaper.

For your file

Read Peta's letter (left). Write a reply to Peta advising her on how to deal with her problem.

Beating the boredom blues

So it's the school holidays, and for once you've got time on your hands. The trouble is: you don't seem to know what to do with it. Samantha Graham suggests 10 things you can do to beat those school holiday boredom blues.

Getting a piece of the action

1. Join the club

Many youth clubs run schemes for teenagers during the holidays, or there may be one being run at your school. Go and find out what's on offer by asking at your local community centre or looking in the community newsletter.

2. Go exploring

Investigate the area where you live. Many people never bother to visit the interesting places in their neighbourhood. Find out about places you can visit and things to see in your area from the local tourist information office or from your local library.

3. Get into shape

Oh no! I hear you groan, but getting fit can be fun. One of the best forms of exercise is swimming, and another is cycling. You don't need to have a 21-gear racer or a mountain bike. You can go at your own speed and explore all those places that you've never got round to seeing.

4. Go green

Contact organisations like Friends of the Earth and see if there are any local environmental schemes that you can get involved in. Or organise your own scheme. For example, get together with some friends and set up a recycling team.

5. Do-it-yourself

Do a deal with your parents. Say that if they let you redesign and redecorate your bedroom and supply you with the materials, you'll do the work yourself. You'll not only learn all about painting and decorating, but you'll also end up with the bedroom you've always wanted.

6. Put it in writing

Get your pen and paper out and get writing. So you never got round to keeping a diary? Well, now's the time to start! Or what about that story that's been lurking at the back of your mind, or the letter you said you'd write to the newspaper to protest about cruelty to animals? Get scribbling.

7. Get crafty

Ask your mum or dad if you can borrow their tools and get out into the shed and make something for yourself. What about a new DVD rack? Raid your money box to buy some of that material you fancied and make yourself something new to wear. Use your practical skills – get crafty!

8. Get in on the act

Join the local drama club and get involved in their productions. You don't fancy acting? Then get a back-stage role, looking after the lighting, painting the scenery, making the costumes or doing the make-up. Or get together with your friends, borrow a video camera and make your own video.

9. Read all about it

Get down to the local library and borrow those expensive books about your hobby that you couldn't afford to buy. Become more of an expert than you already are on the things that really interest you.

10. Get connected

Everyone's been telling you to develop your computer skills. Well, now's your chance. Get on-line and search the net for websites about your favourite subject. You could even design your own blog and make posts for family and friends.

In groups

Discuss Samantha Graham's suggestions. Talk about the ones that appeal to you most and the ones that appeal to you least. Can you suggest other ways of beating boredom and making the most of your leisure time? Keep notes of your ideas and share them in a class discussion.

Choose your exercise

One way you can use your leisure time well is to make sure you get enough exercise. The fitter you are, the more energy you will have. The more energy you have, the more you will be able to get out of life.

True physical fitness is something more than simply being fit to cope with the stresses and strains of everyday life. It consists of three important ingredients: stamina, suppleness and strength – the S-factors.

First and most important is **STAMINA**. This is staying power, endurance, the ability to keep going without gasping for breath. For stamina, you need a well-developed circulation in the heart and lungs so that plenty of vital oxygen is pumped to your working muscles. With increased stamina you have a slower, more powerful heartbeat. You can cope more easily with prolonged or heavy exertion.

Next is **SUPPLENESS** or flexibility. You need to develop maximum range of movement of your neck, spine and joints to avoid spraining ligaments and pulling muscles and tendons. The more mobile you are, the less likely you'll suffer aches and pains brought on by stiffness.

Finally, **STRENGTH**. Extra muscle-power in reserve for those often unexpected heavier jobs. Lifting and shifting need strong shoulder, trunk and thigh muscles. Toned-up tummy muscles help to take the strain.

For your file

"Why do adults make such a fuss about teenagers taking exercise? I can't see the point myself. As far as I'm concerned exercise is a waste of time."
– Sam

Write a reply to Sam, explaining why exercise is important and suggesting the different ways she or he could get some exercise.

In pairs

Talk about the S-factors, discussing why each one is important.

Study the S-factor score chart. Work out a test-yourself quiz, consisting of statements some of which are true and some of which are false, then give the quiz to another group to do. Here is one possible question:

1. Housework builds up your stamina more than digging. True or false?

S-FACTOR SCORE

	Stamina	Suppleness	Strength
Canoeing	***	**	***
Climbing stairs	***	*	**
Cricket	*	**	*
Cycling (hard)	****	**	***
Dancing (ballroom)	*	***	*
Dancing (disco)	***	****	*
Digging (garden)	***	**	****
Football	***	***	***
Gymnastics	**	****	***
Housework (moderate)	*	**	*
Jogging	****	**	**
Judo	**	****	**
Rowing	****	**	****
Swimming (hard)	****	****	****
Tennis	**	***	**
Walking (briskly)	**	*	*
Weightlifting	*	*	****
Yoga	*	****	*

* No real effect   ** Beneficial effect
*** Very good effect   **** Excellent effect

How employment and unemployment affect the local community

When the economy is doing well, and there is full employment, people will have money to spend. They will spend their money on lots of different things, such as buying food, servicing the car or decorating the house. This creates employment for the people who do these jobs. These people in turn earn money, which they can spend elsewhere.

But this cycle can also run in reverse. If people lose their jobs, they will spend less money in the area. A factory closing can be disastrous for a local community, because many people lose their jobs at the same time. Suddenly, there is a lot less money being spent in the local community. This can mean local businesses are forced to close.

Because of this, the government tries to help people stay in work. When a factory closes, it provides help and support for people to find new jobs and stay in the area. Often they have to learn different skills before they can start a new job. This is known as retraining. They may have to attend a course run by a business or a local college.

Key terms

- A person is **employed** when they have a job that they are paid for doing.

- If someone is **unemployed** it means that a person doesn't have a job.

- The **workforce** means people aged between 18 and 65 who can work.

- The Government aims to have 95% of the workforce at work. This is known as **full employment**. Because there are always some people moving from one job to another, it is impossible to have everyone working at once.

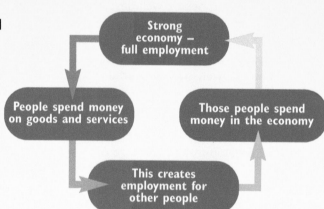

Strong economy – full employment → Those people spend money in the economy → This creates employment for other people → People spend money on goods and services →

Different types of employment

Primary industry

Industry is divided into three main areas. Primary industry involves the production of raw materials through either agriculture, mining or fishing. Farmer, miner and fisherman are all examples of jobs in primary industry. In the past, many people were involved working in this sector of the economy. Today, there are very few, and numbers are declining.

"My name's Frank. I work as a fisherman, based in the port of Grimsby in the north-east of England. It's not like when I started work as a young lad. There used to be a lot more boats here. Part of the problem is over-fishing – people taking too much out of the natural environment so there are fish for today, but not tomorrow. So the EU says we have to be careful how much we fish."

Secondary industry

This is making things out of raw materials – manufacturing. From 1850 to 1950, many people worked in manufacturing industries. Examples include the car industry, which made cars all over the UK. Since the Second World War, the number of people working in manufacturing has dropped dramatically. Many of these jobs have transferred abroad to developing countries such as China and India.

"My name's Joe. I work as a car assembly worker in Coventry – putting headlamps on cars. Things have changed here. The Jaguar factory I work at isn't British any more – it's owned by Tatta, an Indian company. And there's a lot more robots and machines in the factory. Still, it's good to be working on cars. I know many friends who have lost their jobs, and had to retrain to do different work."

Tertiary industry

This consists of jobs in what is known as the service sector. Here, people are providing a service of some kind. Examples of service sector workers include nurses, teachers and call centre advisors. The growth in call centres, where people work together on the telephone, has been so big in recent years that now 1–2% of the entire workforce work in call centres, answering and making telephone calls.

"My name's Liz. I work in a call centre in Poole, dealing with enquiries for Barclays Bank. There's a whole floor of us here – over a hundred people. We all work together to deal with customers' problems. I like working in the service sector. It's good to have contact with lots of different people."

UK employment structure

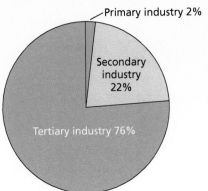

Primary industry 2%

Secondary industry 22%

Tertiary industry 76%

In groups

What does the pie chart tell you about jobs in the UK economy? Where are there fewer jobs? Where are there more jobs? Which sector of the economy can you see yourself working in? Explain why.

For your file

Explain how employment and unemployment affect the local community.
Study the employment listings in your local newspaper. What does this tell you about the jobs that are available in your local area? Write a paragraph for your file explaining what this tells you about the local economy.

Employment for life

In the past, people used to talk about 'employment for life'. The expectation was that when you finished studying you would find a job and that you would do the same job until the day you retired. This was very common for the majority of the 20th century.

Employability for life

Today, people talk about 'employability for life'. Most people will have several different jobs during their working life. The idea is that you may either want to change jobs or be forced to change jobs, for example by being made redundant. Either way, you will still be employable. In other words, you will always be able to get a job.

Jackie's story

"I left school at 16 to become a hairdresser. But after a year's training I decided I didn't like it, and the money didn't pay well enough. So I went back to college and re-trained as a secretary. I worked as a secretary for a local building company for nine years, until I decided to start a family.

Now that my children are at school, I've decided to go back to work. I'm now working in a call centre part time for a local bank. It's good because the hours fit around school hours, so I can still look after my kids.

Eventually, I hope to progress at the call centre. That means becoming a team leader, in charge of a team of six, and eventually a call centre manager."

In groups

Compare the stories of Alfred, Jackie and Mike. Discuss how Jackie's and Mike's experiences are different from Alfred's.

For your file

Imagine you have been asked to write an article for a magazine about working lives and how they have changed in the past 60 years. Interview a number of adults, including some older people, about the jobs they have done during their lives, then draft your article.

Mike's story

"I'm only 22 and I've already have five jobs. I did some temping when I was 16 in a local wood yard and a plastics factory. By the time I was 18, I was working in a bar part time, to help me through college. One summer I did Camp America — working with American school kids providing adventure activities in the holidays.

I've just graduated with a degree in business studies and I'm working in a sales job for a large company. But I don't expect to be doing this for ever. One day I hope to be running my own business."

Alfred's **story**

"I only had one job. At 14, my dad told me it was time to leave school and go down the pit. That was the coal pit. It was the job that most people got in our village. You either went down the pit, or you left for another job.

I worked as a miner all my working life. That's how it was during the last century till the demand for coal dropped and they started closing down most of the mines.

Even my brother Bill, who left the village and went to work in a glass factory, did the same job all his life. It was what you expected.

It's not the same nowadays. I look at my grandchildren and marvel at all the different jobs they have had. Life has certainly changed a lot over the last 50 years."

Transferable skills

While many jobs require some skills that are specific to that particular job, many of the skills you need are the same. As they can be transferred from one job to another, they are known as transferable skills.

A survey of employers showed that they are looking for people who:

- can communicate effectively with colleagues and customers;
- have good interpersonal skills and can work in teams;
- are good at solving problems;
- are numerate and have experience of handling money;
- have good ICT skills;
- are willing and able to learn;
- are flexible in their approach to work.

These skills are transferable between many jobs, so it is important that you develop them while you are at school or college. The more you have developed these skills, the more employable you will be throughout your working life.

In groups

1 Look at the list of jobs (right). Talk about the skills they require. If you were interviewing people for these jobs, which would be the three main transferable skills you would look for in candidates for each job. (Refer back to the list of transferable skills above.)

2 Think about any jobs you have done (for example, a paper round or some voluntary work). What transferable skills did you learn from each job? Which skills would you like to improve in the future?

* sales assistant
* hotel receptionist
* chef
* car mechanic
* bank clerk
* care assistant
* laboratory technician
* call centre worker
* plumber

For your file

How strong are your transferable skills listed above? Rate yourself for each skill on a five-point scale: 5 = excellent, 4 = very good, 3 = good, 2 = not very good, 1 = poor.

Write a short statement, explaining which skills you need to work hard at developing. Say why it is important for you to develop those skills.

Alcohol – the facts

What's all the fuss about?

Alcohol is certainly part of everyday life in our society. But alcohol is a powerful and potentially addictive drug, and you need to be aware of its effects.

In the short term

When you drink, the alcohol is absorbed into your bloodstream. It takes about 5–10 minutes to take effect, but the effects can last for several hours. Of course, how alcohol affects you depends on how much you have drunk, how quickly you've drunk it, how strong it is and whether you've had anything to eat beforehand.

And the effects? Alcohol can make you feel great – relaxed, lively, light-headed and confident. It can also make you feel terrible: sick, dizzy, headachey, clumsy. It's a bit of a myth that alcohol cheers people up – it is actually a depressant and you may end up crying into your drink rather than having a laugh.

Because alcohol reduces self control, there's a real danger of people hurting themselves or others. There's the risk of drinking too much, falling asleep and choking on their own vomit. Then there's the hangover – waking up with a horrible headache but you have to get up and go to school or work.

In the long term

If you're healthy anyway, and if you drink in moderation (at most a couple of drinks a day), you shouldn't have a long-term

Never mix alcohol with other drugs – it can be fatal.

problem with alcohol. But if you drink heavily over a long period you run the risk of brain damage, liver disease (called cirrhosis), mouth and throat cancer, heart problems and stomach ulcers.

People often forget that alcohol is full of calories, hence the 'beer belly' of heavy drinkers. One pint of beer contains about 180 calories.

Alcohol can be addictive and you can become dependent on it. Several hundred thousand people in Britain are thought to be alcoholics. Some of them are not much older than you.

Drink strengths

People often think that certain drinks, such as beer or cider, contain less alcohol than others. In fact, a half pint of ordinary strength beer or cider has about the same amount of alcohol in it as a normal glass of wine or a pub measure of whisky.

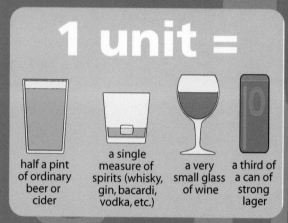

1 unit =

| half a pint of ordinary beer or cider | a single measure of spirits (whisky, gin, bacardi, vodka, etc.) | a very small glass of wine | a third of a can of strong lager |

The alcohol content of drinks is measured in units. The safe limits for adults are considered to be 14 units per week for women and 21 units per week for men. Depending on your age and your size, your safe limits may be much lower.

On average it takes an hour for the alcohol to register in the body, and then one hour per unit of alcohol drunk for it to disappear

Did you know?

It is dangerous to drink when you are pregnant. Heavy drinking can affect the baby's health and weight at birth.

In groups

"*People who don't drink are kill-joys. They just don't know how to have a good time. Why should we take any notice of what they say? The risks of drinking are exaggerated.*" Kirstie (15)

"*I think that people my age who drink are immature. They do it to show off and try to make themselves popular, but they don't impress me when they start throwing up.*" Shareen (14)

Discuss the views of these young people and say why you agree or disagree with them.

Teenage drinking

Alcohol and young people – the law

Buying alcohol You are not allowed to buy alcohol until you are 18. A shopkeeper or pub landlord can be prosecuted for selling alcohol to anyone under 18. If you are under 18 and try to buy or drink alcohol on licensed premises, you can be fined. Anyone who buys you a drink in a bar when you are under 18 is committing an offence. However, if you're over 16, you can be bought some drinks in a restaurant to have with a meal; beer, cider and wine.

Drinking alcohol When you are 14 you are allowed to go into a licensed bar, but it is an offence for you to drink alcohol in a licensed bar if you are under 18. The police can confiscate alcohol from anyone under 18 who is drinking it in a public place. However, it is not illegal for under 18s to drink alcohol either in their own home or someone else's.

Shock tactics in binge-drinking ads

'You wouldn't start a night like this, so why end it that way?' is the message, designed to show the consequences of drinking too much.

One TV ad depicts a young man getting ready for a night out who rips out his ear-ring, smashes a wardrobe door in his face, urinates on his shoes and pours a takeaway down his shirt.

Another shows a young woman arranging vomit in her hair, smudging make-up down her face and ripping her clothes.

The campaign challenges people to think twice about the consequences of losing control.

Binge-drinking not only damages your health but makes you vulnerable to harm.

If you get drunk you are much more likely to be involved in an accident or assault, be charged with a criminal offence, contract a sexually transmitted infection or have an unplanned pregnancy.

In groups

What do the articles suggest are the risks a person runs if they get very drunk? What do you think of people who get very drunk? How would you describe their behaviour – funny? stupid? disgusting? immature?

What is your opinion of someone who deliberately tries to get someone drunk?

In pairs

Study the information on these two pages and produce a true or false quiz, consisting of statements about alcohol and drinking. Then swap your quiz with another pair.

For your file

Design a poster entitled 'Think Before You Drink' to make young people of your age aware of how drinking can affect them.

Problem drinking

Kerry's story

Kerry, 15, started drinking for a laugh with her mates. But now she's relying on it more and more ...

"If you'd said to me a while ago that I'd be drinking most weekends at 14, I'd never have believed you. When I was younger and my mum and dad let me try their drinks, I always thought they were disgusting – I couldn't see why anyone would want to drink them because they tasted so horrible."

Confidence

"That all changed when my mate Ailsa got her brother to buy us some cider one night. We were supposed to be seeing some lads in the park later on and we had it before we met them. Ailsa said it tasted okay and would give us confidence and she was right – I couldn't believe how good it made me feel. I've always been quite a shy and nervous person, but after a few swigs of cider, I felt really good. Ailsa and I were laughing at everything and I became much more loud and confident. I felt really good about myself – much better than I normally did."

"That night we met the lads in the park. Normally, I'd have been so quiet and shy with them, but because I'd had some cider I felt great and I actually got off with James, the boy I'd fancied for ages."

Cider

"After that Ailsa and I would split a bottle of cider between us whenever we were going somewhere, like to a mate's party. Then I started feeling like I needed a drink to get me in the mood for enjoying myself, even if we were just going down the park to hang around. If I haven't had a drink and there are lads there I feel all panicky and shaky and don't usually say much to them."

"I spend a fortune on mints because my mum would kill me if she ever found out that I'm drinking, and all my pocket money seems to go on cider these days. I know I'm probably relying on drink too much now but at least I'm having fun."

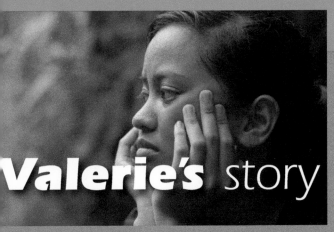

Valerie's story

"My father died when I was nine and I think that was when my mother started drinking heavily. It was a horrific situation because I felt so helpless. I would come home and she'd be sitting in front of the TV completely drunk. Very often there would be no food on the table and no money to buy any because she'd spent it all on drink. Sometimes I'd have to go round to a friend's house and beg them to lend us some money – it was so humiliating."

Gradually her mother's problem became more serious and it was Valerie who had to run the home. "I had two younger brothers to look after as well, which was no joke. I used to come home with heaps of homework only to spend my evenings cooking, cleaning and doing the laundry. It was very difficult because I really wanted to go to university but I couldn't fit in time for studying."

For Valerie, the worst thing was the uncertainty. "I'd never know quite what to expect when I came home. One day I came in and found her rolling around on the kitchen floor, so drunk that she'd wet herself. I had to clean her up and put her to bed like a baby."

Valerie tried everything she could. She joined a local branch of Alateen. She tried to get her mother to join a support group to kick the habit. But although her mother tried to change, the attempts were usually short-lived. "I felt very guilty about it. I began to think that maybe I was to blame for her drinking, and that I had to make her stop. I also felt guilty about wanting to leave and go to college when I knew that there would be no one to look after her or my younger brothers, and I realised that I had to make a difficult choice."

In the end she got a place at a university 20 miles away so she could still live at home. Now 20 and in her second year, she is finding it more and more difficult to keep up with course work and look after the family. "I'm a bit fed up because I am missing out on all the social life and, whenever a guy asks me out, I usually have to turn him down. I sometimes wish that someone would pay attention to me for a change – Mum has always been the centre of attention because of her problem. All I can hope is that one day she will get over this."

In groups

Discuss Kerry's story. Do you think she has a problem or is she just having fun? What would you say to her to persuade her to cut down her drinking?

Discuss the problems that Valerie has had to face because of her mother's alcoholism. What do you learn about what it feels like to have a parent with a drinking problem?

For your file

Study the advice on how to cope. Imagine you write an advice column for a teen magazine. Write your reply to a letter from Tony (13) who lives alone with his father. His father has a drink problem and Tony is trying to cope.

Living with someone who drinks – how to cope

- Look after yourself. Take steps to protect yourself, especially if you think you might be at risk.

- Don't blame yourself for their drinking. Each adult is responsible for themself.

- Don't pour away alcohol unless someone asks you to. Taking alcohol from someone who is already drunk may put you at risk of being hurt.

- Don't cover up or make excuses to other people for their drinking.

- Don't be afraid to voice your concerns when they are sober.

- Tell another adult you trust what's going on. Share the burden.

- Contact Alateen and Al-Anon Family Groups. They are organisations that aim to help families of problem drinkers. Alateen deals specifically with teenagers who have been, or still are, affected by an alcoholic relative. The organisation is completely confidential.

Tel: 020 7407 0215
www.al-anonuk.org.uk/alateen

Change and the school community – the six-term year

Your school is a community of people with a common aim – to provide you with an education that will enable you to make the fullest use of your talents and that will prepare you for life as an adult citizen.

The school community is made up of lots of different groups of people: students, teachers, classroom assistants, administrative staff, care-taking and cleaning staff, parents and governors. Whenever a major change is made – for example, to the size of the school, the hours of the school day or the number of terms in the school year – it will affect all these groups.

A new school year?

Traditionally, the pattern of the school year in England and Wales has been three terms:

■ A long winter term with a week's half-term in the middle, followed by a break of about a fortnight at Christmas.

■ A spring term, varying in length according to the date of Easter, with a week for half-term, followed by a break of about a fortnight over Easter.

■ A summer term with the first half varying in length because of the date of Easter, with a week's half-term, followed by a long summer holiday, often of 7 or 8 weeks.

Some people argue that it would be better to have a six-term year. The six-term year would consist of:

■ Two terms before Christmas;

■ No term longer than 38 days (7 weeks and 3 days);

■ A 2-week October break between terms 1 and 2;

■ A break of 2 weeks over Christmas between terms 2 and 3;

■ Four terms after Christmas of no longer than 6 weeks each;

■ A week's break between terms 3 and 4 and terms 5 and 6 (traditional spring and summer half-term);

■ The break between terms 4 and 5 being fixed each year, instead of varying according to the date of Easter

■ A summer break of always more than 5 weeks.

Longer school days and shorter holidays

In 2013, the Education Secretary Michael Gove suggested that from September 2014 schools should introduce a longer school day, lasting till 4.30 pm, and shorten the summer holiday to 4 weeks. He claimed the changes would improve standards and make life easier for working parents.

Opponents of the proposals argue that longer school days would not improve performances because children, especially younger ones, would become tired and unable to concentrate. It would also mean that children would have less time to do out-of-school activities.

"Not everything they learn stems from bring in a classroom," said Kevin Courtney, deputy secretary of the National Union of Teachers, "We must remember that young people are entitled to a childhood and some time when they can simply relax."

A change for the better?

Here are some reactions to the proposal to change to a six-term year.

"How would everyone manage to fit in their holidays during a shorter summer break? It's hard enough as it is trying to get time off when everyone else wants it."
– Parent

"It would increase the pressure on teachers, who would lose the advantage of having a long block of time in the summer in which to do detailed planning."
– Teacher

"It might ease the frantic scramble there is at the beginning of the autumn term to sort everything out, by spreading things over the year a bit more."
– School secretary

"You don't want to be in school in the summer when it's hot. I'd much rather have a long summer holiday than lots of short breaks throughout the year."
– Student

"I'm all for it. Children get out of the habit of studying during the summer holiday. It's always a fight to get them to do their homework when they go back in the autumn." – Parent

"We do a lot of maintenance work in the summer holidays at present. But we should be able to fit it in whatever the pattern of the school year."
– Caretaker

"Research shows that many children have forgotten what they have learned when they return to school after a six-week break. I think it would help us to improve the school's academic results."
– Governor

In groups

List what you think to be the advantages and disadvantages of having a six-term school year, taking into consideration how it would affect all members of the school community.

Organise a debate on the motion: 'This house believes that a six-term school year is better than a three-term school year.'

In groups

Talk about how your school day is organised. Imagine you have been asked to inquire into ways of changing it. What are the arguments for and against:

a   an earlier start or a later start;

b   longer or shorter morning/afternoon breaks;

c   a longer lunch hour;

d   an earlier or a later finishing time?

Consider other ideas, such as reorganising the lesson timetable so that all the lessons take place on four and a half days -- activities could then be organised on the other half-day to allow students to pursue their own interests. In your discussions, take into consideration how your suggestions would affect the various different members of the school's community.

Decide whether or not you recommend any changes to the school day. Appoint a spokesperson to report your conclusions to the rest of the class in a class discussion.

Participating in the school community

School councils

Most schools have a school council, which exists to let the teachers and headteacher know what students' opinions are on a range of school issues. The school council usually consists of two or three elected representatives from each year group.

Year councils

Because school councils are sometimes dominated by older students, some schools have introduced year councils. The aim of a year council is to give students the opportunity to express opinions on matters of importance to that particular year group.

"Our school council meets once every three weeks. It discusses issues such as the dress code, the use of social areas, charity fundraising and bullying."

Beach Lane School Year 8 Council – constitution

1 The council's purpose is to act as a forum for discussion of school issues relevant to Year 8, and to let the teachers and headteacher know what student opinion is on these issues. The council will also take responsibility for co-operating with year staff in the organisation of one social event per term for Year 8.

2 Membership of the council will consist of three representatives from each class, elected on a termly basis.

3 Meetings will be held once a fortnight. The council members will elect a chair to control the meetings and a secretary who will be responsible for circulating the agenda for each meeting and taking and circulating minutes of meetings.

4 The class representatives will be responsible for giving a report of the council's meetings to their class. Agenda and minutes of meetings will be put up in each classroom.

5 The Year 8 council will elect two of its members to be members of the school council, with responsibility for raising issues on behalf of Year 8 students at school council meetings.

6 The chair, secretary and school council representatives will be responsible for taking up matters raised at council meetings with the year head and other teachers, and for reporting back on such matters to the Year 8 council.

7 The head of year will attend all council meetings as an observer and both they and the other year staff will be available as required to offer support and advice to council members and to assist in the settlement of disputes.

In groups

Imagine that elections are about to be held for class representatives to the Year 8 council. Choose one of the group to stand as a candidate. Together draft a statement of the issues you think the Year 8 council should take up for your candidate to present to the rest of the class to explain why she or he should be elected. Then listen to the various candidates' statements and hold a mock election to elect two representatives.

For your file

Write a letter to the school council on a Year 8 issue (for example, the lack of a social area for Year 8 students at break times; the need to improve the provision of lockers and locker space for Year 8 students; the amount of bullying of Year 8s by older students), asking the school council to discuss the issue and take it up with the teaching staff.

The Henry Box School – school uniform

It is the policy of the school that all students in Years 7–11 wear the agreed uniform. Our school uniform helps to create a smart appearance, a sense of belonging from a common identity and a feeling of pride in The Henry Box School. The full uniform must be worn to and from school.

THE MAIN SCHOOL UNIFORM

School sweatshirt – this is central to our uniform and all students will wear these.

Trousers and skirts – black (skirts around the knee; trousers should be no longer than shoes to avoid danger of tripping and should not be of excessive width) and traditional style (not denim or cord).

Shirt – white formal 'school shirt' (vests or T-shirts must not show at the neck, and shirts must be tucked in unless it is a fitted formal shirt with collar for girls).

Socks – plain dark or white.

Tights – plain black.

Shoes – black, plain, low heeled (no higher than 6cm) of a sensible design.

ADDITIONAL ITEMS

Outside coats – It is important that students have a coat that is warm and weatherproof and is of a normal style. The school reserves the right not to accept a coat if it would give a poor impression of The Henry Box School. Unacceptable coats include leather, simulated leather, suede, denim, tracksuit tops and coats with offensive logos. Unacceptable coats will be confiscated and the student provided with a suitable coat for the day.

Scarves – these may be worn in poor weather conditions outdoors.

Hats – in the summer in sunny weather only, plain navy blue hats (non-woollen) are permitted. During the winter in cold weather only, woollen hats are allowed. Hats/caps may be worn outdoors only. A small designer logo is allowed but football hats or those with large logos are not permitted. If hats are worn inappropriately or are of an unacceptable design or colour, they will be confiscated.

Trainers – these may be worn during sporting activities or on the tennis courts or field, during break and lunchtime or curricular activities that require them. They should not be worn around school or on the way to and from school.

Jewellery – students may wear a wristwatch, a flat ring, a crucifix or similar. One small ear stud per ear is allowed but studs in other parts of the body are not permitted. It is not permitted to have forbidden items of jewellery covered by a plaster.

Hair styles – The school reserves the right not to accept a hair style that may give a poor impression of the school. Only hair dyed a natural colour is permitted. If a student dyes their hair an unnatural/bright colour, they will be isolated from lessons or sent home until the hair is returned to a natural colour.

Make-up – not allowed in Key Stage 3. In Key Stage 4, discreet make-up is allowed. Coloured nail varnish is not permitted.

In groups

Imagine that your school is currently revising its dress code. Compare your school's dress code with that of The Henry Box School (above). Suggest how you would like to alter your current Year 8 uniform requirements. Make notes of your views, then share your ideas in a class discussion.

Organising a social event

This page explains how your class can work together to organise a social event.

There are various types of social event you could organise.

- An ice-skating trip
- A theatre trip to a play, a concert or show
- A trip to an international sports event
- A Year 8 disco
- A visit to a theme park

In groups

Discuss your ideas for a social event. Then share your ideas in a class discussion and hold a vote to decide what type of social event your class would like to organise.

Planning the event

Make a list of all the jobs that will have to be done in order for the event to take place. Then, share your ideas and draw up a complete list of everything that needs to be done (see class 8L's list, right).

A planning committee

Once you have decided on the event and listed the jobs to be done, appoint a planning committee. The advantage of having a planning committee is that you can arrange for it to meet regularly to check that everything has been done and to deal with any problems that may arise.

Reviewing the event

After the event, hold a class discussion. Talk about what went well, the problems you faced while organising it, and how you coped with them. What were the strengths and weaknesses of how you organised the event? What lessons did you learn? How would you do things differently, if you were to organise a similar event in the future?

8L ice-skating trip

Checklist of tasks for planning committee

✔ Choose date and check school calendar to check that it doesn't clash with any other event.

✔ Contact ice-rink to check opening times, cost of entrance, skate hire and what refreshments are on sale.

✔ Contact bus company to check availability and cost of coach, and book coach.

✔ Advertise the trip and get people to sign up for it.

✔ Check health and safety regulations to ensure that there are enough adults available to come on trip.

✔ Send out letter to inform parents of arrangements for trip.

✔ Arrange for collection of money to pay for the coach.

Planning a budget for your trip

The cost of the coach

The cost of a coach will vary depending on the size of the coach you require and how far the journey is, for example, from the school to the ice-rink. Also, different companies may charge different prices.

The 8L planning committee decided to get quotes from three different coach companies. They found that the cost of hiring a 29 or 30-seater coach for the evening varied from £250 with one company to £300 with another. One of the companies also asked for a £50 deposit when the booking was confirmed.

All three companies had a cancellation policy. For example, the Buzz-A-Bus company would charge 25% of the total cost of £250 (£75) if the booking was cancelled 28 days before, rising to 100% if the booking was cancelled on the day of the trip.

The committee worked out that if they booked a 29-seater coach for £250, then 25 children could pay £10 each for the coach and four adults accompanying them.

The 8L committee asked the school council for a loan of £250 to pay for the coach, in case the trip had to be cancelled due to unforeseen circumstances. The committee had to agree to organise a fundraising event to raise money to repay the loan, if necessary.

Entrance to the ice-rink

The committee contacted the ice-rink and found that the entrance fee (including skate-hire) varied according to the times of the sessions. For the early evening sessions, the entrance fees for under 17s were £4.60. Entrance for the 2-hour Friday night disco was £7 with no reductions for under 17s.

When they asked about discounts for party bookings, they were told that for a party of 29 the entrance fee to the disco session would be reduced to £6.00.

After consulting with the rest of the class, the committee chose to go to the disco evening and sent out a letter saying that the trip would cost £10 for the coach and £6 for entrance to the ice-rink.

Work out a budget for a class trip, similar to 8L's ice-skating trip.

If someone is ill and unable to go on a trip after they have paid for a place, would you refund their money? Discuss the arguments for and against offering a refund.

Facts and opinions

Whenever you discuss an issue, it is important to listen to other people's views, to consider their arguments and, if they are convincing, to change your mind about what you think.

In order to be able to judge the strength of other people's arguments, you need to be able to distinguish whether what they are saying is a **fact** or an **opinion**.

A **fact** is a true statement. It can be about an event or thing that is known to have happened, or about something that can be shown to be true by experience or observation. For example:

"Elephants require vast spaces to roam, socialize, and express their natural behavior."

An **opinion** is a judgement or belief. It is a statement of a point of view based on what a person thinks and feels. For example:

"Elephants should not be kept in zoos."

When someone is explaining the reasons why they hold an opinion, they often use a fact to support their view. For example:

"Elephants should not be kept in zoos because they require vast spaces to roam, socialize, and express their natural behavior."

Forming your opinion

Before you take part in any discussion ...

Find out the facts. For example, by reading articles on the subject or looking for information in the library and on the internet. Check that any information you already have is correct and up-to-date.

Identify what the main issue is and what different opinions people have. Note down the arguments that are used for and against a particular point of view and any facts and examples used to support those arguments.

Decide what your opinion is. Make a list of arguments why you hold that opinion.

During the discussion ...

Listen to what other people have to say. Note down any new arguments that people introduce, or any key facts you learn from them.

If you find other people's opinions convincing, be prepared to alter your own opinion. However, if you think you are right, don't be pressurised into changing your opinion just because other people don't agree with you. Each of you has a right to your own opinion and you should agree to differ.

In pairs

Study the list of statements (below) and decide which are facts and which are opinions.

1 Tongue-piercing can cause infections.

2 Body-piercing improves your looks.

3 Animals should be left to die completely natural deaths.

4 Vets can advise you whether or not your pet is terminally ill.

5 There are a number of decisions that 12-year-olds cannot make for themselves.

6 12-year-old children are good at making decisions.

7 There is too much violence in television programmes.

8 Some popular cartoon series contain scenes of violence.

9 Many roads get congested around the time that schools start and finish.

10 Pupils who live within 3 miles of their school should always walk or cycle to school.

Body-piercing – what's your verdict?

Should body-piercing be banned?

NO says Kit, 16

"I can't believe everyone makes such a big deal about body-piercing when it's not hurting anyone except the person who gets it done.

"It looks good and original. The trouble is that parents completely freak when you say you want one because they think of people with piercings all over their body. I would never do that. All I want is a single stud in my eyebrow, which is totally different.

"It annoys me that people with piercings get a bad reputation, too. People think that you're a thug. That's stupid. Quite a few of my friends have had their belly pierced or a stud put in their tongue. It doesn't make them bad people; it doesn't change their personality.

"Safety is something I think about. But unless you're stupid enough to do one yourself, the risks are low. All the proper shops are hygienic so you're more likely to get knocked down by a bus than get an infection."

YES says Kit's mother, Sarah

"I know that piercing is fashionable but it looks so ugly and primitive. I don't want people to judge Kit badly because he's got a piece of metal sticking out of his face.

"If Kit has an eyebrow pierced he'll have to look at it every day of his life – and I'm worried that he'll regret that later on. It's all very well saying that it's not forever, but if he took it out he could be left with a bad scar.

"I don't even want to think about the health risks. Kit tells me piercing shops sterilise their equipment, but there are no guarantees. I'm not stupid. I know there are still a lot of places that are really unhygienic. It's easy to get an infection from a dirty piercing gun."

Sickening sight!

"I think the whole idea of body-piercing is quite sick! Who would want to walk down the street with their nose, eyebrow and other body parts pierced?

Ear-piercing is fine but some people go way over the top by piercing other parts of their body. Several girls in my school think that having a pierced belly button is cool. No chance!"

"There is no official age limit under which you are not allowed to do body-piercing, but we suggest members use their own ethics and morals. We would support some sort of legislation or guidelines."

– Zoe Rockliffe, secretary of the European Professional Piercing Association

On your own

Study the information and views about body-piercing given in the articles on this page. Make notes on the facts and opinions they contain. Form your own opinion about body-piercing and identify the arguments you are going to use to support your opinion.

In groups

Discuss your views on body-piercing.

Dentists warn of piercing perils

Tongue-piercing can cause infections, interfere with breathing, damage teeth and lead to speech impediments, say dentists.

"People having tongue-piercings are putting not just their oral health, but their general health at risk – and we strongly advise people not to," said Dr Geoff Craig of the British Dental Association.

"If people insist on having piercings, they should ensure that

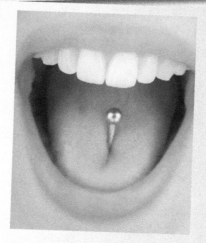

the equipment is sterilised properly and that the stud is made of gold, surgical steel or titanium."

For your file

Write a short statement, expressing your opinion on body-piercing, explaining why you have or have not changed your mind as a result of the discussion.

73

Debating the issue

A debate is a formal discussion in which two opposing arguments are put forward.

The rules of debating

The meeting is opened by the **chair** – the person who controls the meeting and decides who will speak and when. To start the meeting, the chair reads out the **motion** to be debated. The motion is the viewpoint that people will argue for or against. It is presented in a formal way which begins: 'This house believes that ...'

The debate begins with a speech in favour of the motion. The person who speaks first in favour of the motion is called the **proposer**.

Then there is a speech against the motion by a person called the **opposer**.

The chair then declares the motion **open to the floor**. This means that anyone in the audience may now speak either for or against the motion. Anyone who wishes to speak raises their hand, and the chair asks them to speak in turn.

There are then two further speeches – one in favour of and one against the motion. The people who give these speeches are called **seconders**.

After a suitable time to allow as many people as possible to express their views, the chair invites the main speakers to **sum up**. The opposer gives a summary of the main arguments why people should vote against the motion, and the proposer gives a summary of the main arguments why they should vote for the motion.

A **vote** is then organised. The chair reads out the motion and asks 'all those in favour' to raise their hands. They are counted, and then 'all those against' are asked to raise their hands. After they are counted, the chair asks those who wish to **abstain** to raise their hands and the abstentions are counted. (You may wish to abstain for a number of reasons, either because you cannot make up your mind or because you do not agree with either of the views people have expressed.)

Organise your own debate

Either choose your own motion or organise a debate on one of these:

1 This house believes that all animals have the right to die naturally.

2 This house believes that children should be allowed to wear what they like to school.

3 This house believes that the monarchy is out of date and should be abolished.

The chair announces the **result** of the vote and declares that the motion has 'been carried' or 'passed' (the house agrees with motion) or 'defeated' (the house disagrees with the motion).

Writing a speech

There are a number of techniques you can use when writing a speech in order to make it more effective. The advice below is from a helpsheet that a teacher gave to a class who were going to debate the motion, 'This house believes that people who aren't vegetarians are selfish and cruel.'

In pairs

Research the topic, to find out the facts and what the arguments are for and against the issue that is being debated. Then form your opinions. Tell each other which side of the argument you support and draft your speech.

Show your speech to your partner and each make any suggestions you can think of to improve it.

Tips on writing a speech

Grab their attention *Make sure you start with a statement or question that will capture the audience's attention.* **For example:**
'What's wrong with eating meat? 90% of us do. So why should we feel guilty?'

Use facts and statistics *Support your statements with statistics and examples. This strengthens your arguments.* **For example:**
'As many as 90% of battery hens are unable to walk properly.'

Include 'lists of three' *Statements that list things in threes are more likely to hold the audience's attention and stick in their minds.* **For example:**
'Vegetarianism is cruelty-free, environmentally friendly and healthy.'

Use alliteration *A statement that includes a number of words starting with the same letter is likely to be more memorable.* **For example:**
'It's time to stop the senseless slaughter.'

Refer to personal experiences *This suggests you really know what you are talking about.* **For example:**
'I've seen pictures of calves, only a few days old …'

Include questions *These can have a dramatic effect, particularly if they are questions that do not require an answer (these are called rhetorical questions).* **For example:**
'Isn't it obvious that a meat-free diet is better?'

Involve the audience *Addressing the audience directly can help to get them on your side.* **For example:**
'How would you like to spend your life cooped up in a cage?'

'Set them up and knock them down' *This is a particularly effective way of undermining the opposition's arguments.* **For example:**
'What I can't stand about most so-called vegetarians is their hypocrisy. They claim that they don't eat meat to stop animals suffering, yet they go on eating other animal products like eggs and cheese.'

End emphatically *Make sure you end your speech on a high note.* **For example:**
'Whenever you eat meat you're taking the food out of someone else's mouth. If everyone in the world was to become a vegetarian, there'd be enough food for everybody.'

Some young people enter into sexual relationships and have sex without thinking about the consequences. The aim of this unit is to make you aware of what is involved in having a sexual relationship and of the steps you can take to avoid an unwanted pregnancy and to avoid catching a sexually transmitted infection.

Sex and contraception ...
Your questions answered

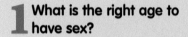

1 What is the right age to have sex?

In Britain it is illegal to have sex under the age of 16.

We all know that some people are very mature at 16 and some are still years away from forming serious relationships. The choice and risks are yours to take, but what's revealing is that the more teenagers know about sex, the longer they wait to do it. Young people who are given frank sex education from an early age find it easier to talk openly with parents and teachers.

Make up your own mind, don't bow to peer pressure and get all the facts and info you need to make informed and safe decisions about your own sex life – then you'll know when the time is right.

2 Who should I talk to about contraception?

The first person you should speak to is the person you're planning to have sex with. This should be something they have to worry about too. If you're counting on acting as a couple then you should sort out contraception together. That could mean they come along to the doctor's with you to lend a bit of support or maybe they're the one who buys the condoms.

3 What if I'm underage and I want contraceptive advice?

Most doctors will be understanding about what you want and will treat your case in confidence. You can double-check about confidentiality beforehand if you don't want your parents to know that you need birth control (see point 4). What you'll find is that most medical staff would rather see you taking a sensible view towards contraception than coming in a few months later asking for a pregnancy test.

4 Can my doctor tell my parents I'm having sex?

This is still very much up to the individual doctor, but most GPs now agree that young people under 16 can see them for contraceptive advice without parental consent. If you are not sure your doctor offers this service then you can phone reception and ask if they provide under-16s this sort of treatment. If you don't feel confident enough to go there then try making an appointment at a family planning clinic.

5 Is the pill foolproof?

The pill is one of the most reliable forms of contraception, but only if you follow the instructions very carefully. If you skip pills or vary the times when they are taken then you reduce the effectiveness.

Contraceptive injections, condoms, implants and patches are alternative options to taking the pill.

6 What is emergency contraception?

Some people still refer to emergency contraception as the morning-after pill – this is because it can be taken up to 72 hours after unprotected sex has taken place, but is less effective after the first 24 hours. If you think you need emergency contraception, make an appointment with your doctor or visit a pharmacy.

Did you know?
The average age when men and women have sex for the first time is now 17.

The rhythm method

This works on the principle that there are certain days within a girl's cycle when she can have sex without getting pregnant. She would need to have extremely regular periods to work out fertile and infertile days. It also means having to carefully plan sex. On top of all this, this method does not offer protection from HIV and STIs (Sexually Transmitted Infections).

Withdrawal

This is not a reliable form of contraception. Withdrawal is when a boy removes his penis from a girl's vagina before he ejaculates. It's a very risky method because sperm often does leak out before ejaculation. It's impossible to control this – so don't believe any boy who says he can stop it happening.

I'm worried about protection

"I'm 13 and I'm going out with a boy. Last weekend we were in his bedroom and we ended up on the bed. We would have gone all the way if I hadn't said I was on my period. I'm very worried about contraception. I overheard him talking to his best mate saying that we were going to have sex and that we didn't need to use contraception. I don't know what to do. I'm scared to say anything, but I don't want to end up pregnant."

Tricia Kreitman says:

Having sex without a condom or any other form of contraception means one thing – you will get pregnant, probably quite quickly.

I don't think you should have sex with him at all. This boy's a real idiot if he's bragging to his friends that he's going to get you into bed. He seems to see not wearing a condom as some kind of macho statement, but in reality it's stupid and cowardly.

I think you're both too young to have sex – the fact you can't discuss contraception shows this. Legally you're still 3 years under the age of consent and, if he's older than you, he could get into real trouble.

But more importantly, I can see that you are likely to get hurt. I don't think this boy's worth the trouble. He sees you as a trophy or something to brag about rather than someone he's in love with. Please give it more time. Don't do something you might regret.

In groups

'Setting the age of consent at 16 is wrong.' Discuss this view. What are the arguments for and against:
a) raising the age of consent to 18; b) lowering the age of consent to 14?

Sexual rights and responsibilities

In any sexual relationship you have rights and responsibilities.

Your sexual responsibilities

1 You should always consider the feelings of your partner.

The key to a happy relationship is considering the feelings of your partner. When you are sensitive to his or her moods, likes and dislikes, you can build trust and learn to relax with each other. So if your partner is upset about something and wants to talk rather than kiss, put your own wishes aside for the moment and tend to their needs.

2 You should never pressurise someone to have sex.

Pressurising someone to have sex is pointless because no amount of pressure is going to create desire where there wasn't any before. If you are a boy, you should never try to force a girl to have sex with you. Even if you genuinely think a girl intends to make love and are surprised when she won't, you shouldn't pressurise her.

To use any kind of advantage or physical pressure to force a person to have sex is assault.

3 You should respect your partner.

Sex can make you feel vulnerable, especially when you're new to it. That is why good sexual relationships require trust between the partners. If a boy or girl has told you secrets, declared love for you, or made some kind of love with you, you should never make fun of him or her for it. When people have been intimate with you they have made themselves vulnerable to you. Don't betray them.

4 You should share the responsibility for birth control and sexual health with your partner.

Part of respecting someone and being considerate of their feelings is being concerned over the consequences of your sexual relationship together. With the increase of sexual diseases, especially AIDS, you have a right to know if your partner is healthy. You have a responsibility to avoid sex if you have a sexual disease.

The responsibility for birth control belongs to both partners.

Your sexual rights

1 You have a right to enjoy sex.

When there's a lot of talk about sexual abuse, it's sometimes hard to remember that sex itself is a beautiful, natural experience – or it should be.

2 You have a right to wait until you're ready for sex.

One of the main ways to guarantee that you will enjoy sex is to wait until you're ready. Don't make yourself start having sex before you really want to just to please a partner or keep up with the crowd.

3 You always have a right to say no.

Your right to say no never changes whatever the circumstances. If someone's spent money on you, taken you out, or given you presents, you don't owe them even as much as a kiss. Even if you've promised to have sex and then changed your mind, you have a right to say no. Your body is not a bargaining chip and you are not for sale.

4 You have a right to be respected.

No one should tell you they don't respect you because of your sexual activities, or pressurise you because of them.

5 You have a right to say yes to some sexual activities and no to others.

Just because you've become physically intimate with someone doesn't mean you have to do anything you don't want to. If you've almost gone all the way but haven't, you aren't obliged to. If anyone tells you that you've gone too far to stop, don't believe them.

Where to go for advice

If you need help or advice on contraception or sexual health, there should be a clinic in your area that runs sessions for young people. Ask at a health centre or look it up online.

Confidential helplines
• Brook 0808 802 1234 • Childline 0800 1111/www.childline.org.uk

Sex myths

Everybody's doing it

Everybody's talking about it, but not everybody's doing it. If you are surrounded by friends who boast about having sex, take what they say with a pinch of salt. For starters, sex isn't something to show off about. It's a private thing between two people.

Having sex means you are grown-up

Sex doesn't have anything to do with being grown-up, mature or adult. In fact, lots of adults make mistakes when it comes to sex. They rush into things, and regret it in the same way that young people might do. Being older doesn't mean you're wiser, in the same way that doing adult things doesn't make you an adult.

Sex strengthens a relationship

Sex only strengthens a relationship that's already strong. That means a relationship where you know and care about each other, where you've discussed things, and taken the right precautions. If you haven't done these things, sex will only weaken your relationship.

In groups

People have different views about what is acceptable in a sexual relationship. On your own, study the list (below) and decide which types of behaviour are acceptable and which are unacceptable. Then share your views in a group discussion.

What is acceptable in a sexual relationship?

1 To do things to please your boy/girlfriend.
2 To tell your friends all about what you and your partner do together.
3 To stop seeing a friend if your boy/girlfriend doesn't like them.
4 To have a relationship with someone of a different religion.
5 To lie to your parent(s) or friends about where you are going and what you are doing.
6 To have sex without being in love.
7 To tell lies to your boy/girlfriend, if you think the truth might hurt them.
8 To have sex because one person wants to.
9 To hit each other.
10 To argue a lot.
11 To disagree about issues.
12 To go out with your friends without your boy/girlfriend.
13 To be attracted to other people while you are in a relationship.
14 To be sexually faithful to one another.
15 To let one partner take full responsibility for taking precautions.
16 To change your mind about doing something that you have made a promise to do.

Parliament in focus

The House of Commons and the House of Lords are made up of different groups of people and have different functions.

The House of Commons

The House of Commons consists of 650 MPs, who are the elected representatives of the people of Great Britain. Most MPs belong to a political party. The main purpose of the House of Commons is to make laws.

How a law is made

A proposal for a new law is called a bill. Bills are usually introduced by the government, although some are proposed by individual MPs. The flow-chart below shows how each bill has to pass through a number of stages before it becomes an Act of Parliament. Each bill has to pass through three 'readings' in both the House of Commons and the House of Lords.

From bill to act

Drafting
A public bill is drawn up carefully in written form, and discussed by the Cabinet.

First reading
The bill is published (printed so that it can be examined), usually for the House of Commons first. There is no debate.

Second reading
A vote is taken a few weeks later. If a majority approves of the bill, it is passed.

Parliamentary committee
Amendments (changes) to the bill are discussed and made.

Report stage
The committee sends a report to the House of Commons with all the amendments. These are approved or changed.

Third reading
Again, there is a debate on the bill, and a vote is taken.

Royal assent
A royal commission gives the bill royal assent if it has been approved by the House of Commons and the House of Lords.

Act of Parliament
The bill becomes law, and is known as an Act of Parliament.

John Bercow, the Speaker makes sure that business is conducted according to the rules of Parliament. It is their job to keep order and to decide whose turn it is to speak.

What happens in the House of Commons?

Parliament meets about 160 days a year. The first 45 to 50 minutes of each sitting, except on Fridays, is known as Question Time. Ministers take it in turns to answer questions about the work of their departments. Once a week the Prime Minister answers questions. After Question Time, a minister may make a statement on an important issue or outline a new policy, explaining the reasons for it.

Next there is a session called 'public business'. This includes dealing with the various stages of bills and the main debate. The debate may be on a proposal for a new law, or it may be a general debate on a subject such as the economy or defence.

At the end of the debate a vote is taken. All the political parties appoint some of their MPs to act as party 'whips'. Whips are a party's "enforcers," who offer inducements and threaten punishments for party members to make sure that they vote according to the official party policy.

Whips are a party's "enforcers", who offer inducements and threaten punishments for party members to make sure that they vote according to the official party policy. It is also the job of the whips to ensure that MPs from their party are present when a vote is to be taken.

For your file

Make notes on what you learn from this page about: a) how the House of Commons is made up; b) how its business is conducted; c) how a law is made.

Use the library or the internet to find out about how MPs vote and where people sit in the debating chamber. Add this information to your notes.

The House of Lords

The House of Lords has existed since the 1300s. It has three main functions:

- It examines and revises bills that pass through the House of Commons.

- It holds debates on matters of public interest which are not heard in the House of Commons.

- It acts as the final court of appeal in the British judicial system: the law lords (judges) can make a final judgement on any court decision.

In 2014, there were 778 members of the House of Lords. The majority were life peers, who are appointed by the sovereign on the advice of the prime minister. The others were hereditary peers (who had inherited from their families the right to sit in the House of Lords), 26 "Lords Spiritual" (archbishops and bishops) of the Church of England and 12 law lords.

Reforming the Lords

In 1997, there were 750 hereditary peers with the right to vote in the House of Lords. The government passed an act in 1999 allowing only 92 of the hereditary peers to vote. These 'voting peers' were elected by all the hereditary peers.

The reform of the House of Lords was to be a two-stage process. In the second stage, it was proposed that 80% of the House of Lords was to be elected by the public and the number of peers was to be reduced to 450. However, plans to reform the House of Lords were abandoned in 2012, because David Cameron's Conservative Party rejected the proposed reforms, although their Liberal Democrat coalition partners supported it (see page 82 for more information on the coalition government).

In groups

Some people argue that the current reform of the House of Lords has not gone far enough.

"Its members are not elected by anybody. It should be abolished and replaced by a new 'House of Representatives' elected by the people, as the House of Commons is."

"No hereditary peers should be allowed to vote in the House of Lords."

"Why should ex-government ministers still have a say in running the country by being made life peers? The whole system is wrong."

Others argue that the House of Lords should have been left as it was.

"The present system has worked well for centuries. It was ridiculous to change something out of envy and spite."

"The House of Lords does a good job. It gives the opportunity for second thoughts on new laws. On average, 95% of amendments to bills made in the Lords are accepted in the Commons. We shouldn't have changed things for change's sake."

Discuss these views. Then share your ideas in a class discussion and hold a vote on whether you think the House of Lords should be reformed.

The government in action

The government is the group of people who manage the nation's affairs. After a general election, the government is formed by the leader of the political party with the most MPs, who becomes Prime Minister. If their party does not have an overall majority in the House of Commons, they may come to an agreement with another party to form a coalition government. This happened in 2010 when the Conservative Party, led by David Cameron, formed a coalition government with the Liberal Democrats, led by Nick Clegg.

The Prime Minister appoints a team of about 100 ministers to run the country. Each minister is responsible for a particular aspect of government, such as transport or education.

The Cabinet

The Cabinet is the name given to a group of senior ministers who meet to decide the government's policy on all major issues. Four of the most important members of the Cabinet are:

- the Home Secretary, who is in charge of the police force, prisons and keeping law and order;

- the Foreign Secretary, who is responsible for Britain's dealings with other countries;

- the Chancellor of the Exchequer, who is responsible for the nation's finances;

- the Justice Secretary and Lord Chancellor, who is responsible for the administration of the law.

What are political parties?

A political party is a collection of people at local, regional and national levels who broadly share the same views. They group together so that they can pool their resources and give themselves a better chance of gaining power.

Most political parties are coalitions, involving several different types of political opinion. For example, the Labour Party is a coalition of trade unionists, Fabians, social democrats and socialists.

Most MPs are members of the three main political parties – the Conservative Party, the Labour Party or the Liberal Democrats. At the 2010 election, Caroline Lucas became the first Green Party MP.

The opposition

All MPs who do not belong to the political party that forms the government are called opposition MPs. The political party with the largest number of opposition MPs becomes the official opposition. Its leader is known as the Leader of the Opposition, and they appoint members of their party to act as spokespeople on particular matters. This group of MPs is known as the shadow cabinet.

In pairs

Compile a 'Who's who in Parliament'. List the names of:

- the Prime Minister and the Cabinet;

- the Leader of the Opposition and the shadow cabinet;

- the leaders of all the other main political parties.

The finances of government

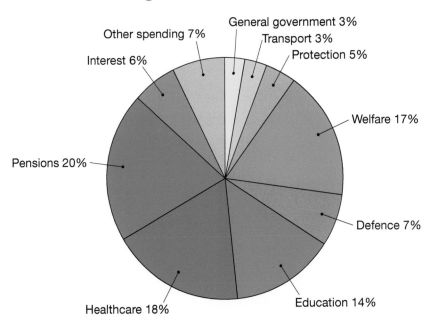

Other spending 7%
Interest 6%
General government 3%
Transport 3%
Protection 5%
Welfare 17%
Pensions 20%
Defence 7%
Healthcare 18%
Education 14%

Controlling finance

It is the duty of the House of Commons, on behalf of the people, to make sure that taxes are not raised without good reason. The budget proposals are set out in a bill and are then examined and discussed carefully, before becoming law in the Finance Act.

The House of Commons has to give its approval, before any money can be spent by the government. So the government has to present what each department estimates its spending will be. The House has to agree these estimates before the departments are given any money.

The House of Commons also checks that the departments spend the money as they said they would and examines any cases of overspending. This is done by a committee known as the Public Accounts Committee.

How the government raises money

Each year the government has to raise money in order to pay for things that are paid for by the state, such as the health service, education, transport, defence and social security. The government raises this money through taxes. Taxes can be raised on a variety of items, for example on people's incomes, on the goods they buy or on the profits made by companies.

Each year the government announces its plans for any new taxes or changes to existing taxes in a statement called the budget. The budget is usually made in the spring, when the Chancellor of the Exchequer presents a 'budget statement' to the House of Commons.

How the government spends money

Every year the government also decides how much money it will spend in each government department. There are fifteen main departments in the government, including the Treasury (which controls the budgets of all the departments), the Home Office (which looks after law and order), the Foreign Office, Education and Employment, Defence, Social Security and the Department of the Environment. The pie-chart (above) shows the percentage of projected spending in each area for 2013.

In groups

Study the articles on this page and discuss what you learn from them about: **a)** how the government raises money; **b)** what it spends money on; **c)** how government finances are controlled.

In pairs

Study the information on pages 80–85 and make a short dictionary of parliamentary terms. Here is the start of such a dictionary:

Act of Parliament: A bill that has passed through all its parliamentary stages and become a law.

How MPs are elected

General elections

An election to choose the members of a new Parliament is called a **general election**. A general election has to be held at least once every five years.

The Prime Minister can call a general election at any time. Sometimes a Prime Minister finds that they can no longer get Parliament's support for their policies, and so is forced to resign and to call an election. Usually, the Prime Minister tries to call an election at a time when the government is popular, in the hope that it will get re-elected.

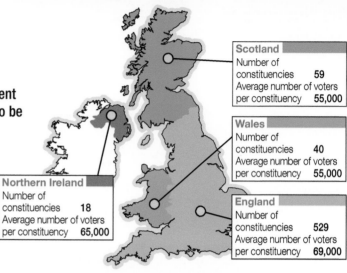

Scotland
Number of constituencies 59
Average number of voters per constituency 55,000

Wales
Number of constituencies 40
Average number of voters per constituency 55,000

Northern Ireland
Number of constituencies 18
Average number of voters per constituency 65,000

England
Number of constituencies 529
Average number of voters per constituency 69,000

Election campaigns

During the election campaign each party issues a **manifesto** – a pamphlet explaining its policies. The candidates hold public meetings and tour the constituency to try to persuade people to vote for them.

There are strict controls on the amount each individual candidate can spend on election expenses. There are also restrictions on the number and length of election broadcasts on radio and television. The amount of time given to each party is agreed between the parties and the broadcasting authorities. For the first time at the 2001 general election the amount a political party could spend was limited. The limit was £320 million.

The right to vote

Most people over the age of 18 are able to vote. The most notable exceptions are people in prison, members of the House of Lords and the criminally insane.

Candidates

Anyone aged over 21 can be a candidate for election to Parliament. Your name has to be put forward by ten electors, but you don't have to be born or live in the constituency. Most candidates belong to a political party.

Constituencies

For election purposes, Britain is divided into 646 separate areas, known as **constituencies**. All the adults who live in a constituency vote to choose one person to represent them in Parliament.

The size of constituencies varies as does the number of voters per constituency. Country constituencies are larger than town constituency. It is proposed that in future the number of voters should be the same in each constituency and that the number of constituencies should be reduced to 600. However, these changes have been postponed until after the 2015 election.

Secret ballot

Voting is by **secret ballot** and takes place at a **polling station**. Each voter is given a piece of paper called a ballot paper, on which there is a list of the candidates' names. The voter puts a cross against the candidate they support, then puts the ballot paper in a sealed box.

By-elections

When an MP dies or resigns, and no general election is due, an election is held in that constituency only. This is called a **by-election**. During a by-election, the amount a candidate can spend on the election is four times the amount they could spend in a general election.

Who becomes an MP?

MPs come from all sorts of backgrounds, but the average age of MPs in the 2010 Parliament was 50.

The youngest MP was Pamela Nash, the Liberal MP for Airdrie and Shotts, who was 28. There are many more men than women in Parliament. After the 2010 General Election 503 men and 147 women were elected. There were 27 MPs from ethnic minority backgrounds.

What do MPs do?

MPs split their time between working in Parliament itself, working in the constituency that elected them and working for their political party. Some MPs from the governing party (or parties) become government ministers with specific responsibilities in certain area, such as health or defence.

Working in Parliament

When Parliament is sitting (meeting), MPs generally spend their time working in the House of Commons. This can include raising issues affecting their constituents, attending debates and voting on new laws. Most MPs are also members of committees, which look at issues in detail, from government policy and new laws, to wider topics like human rights.

Working in their constituency

In their constituency, MPs often hold a 'surgery' in their office, where local people can come along to discuss any matters that concern them. MPs also attend functions, visit schools and businesses, and generally try to meet as many people as possible. This gives MPs further insight and context into issues they may discuss when they return to Westminster.

In groups

"It is wrong that Parliament is dominated by white males, many of whom are over 50. We need more women in Parliament, more young people and more people from ethnic minorities."

Discuss this view. What can be done to increase the number of women, young people and ethnic minority MPs?

Is the present voting system fair?

When the votes at a general election have been counted, the person with the highest number of votes is declared the winner and becomes the MP for that constituency. This system of choosing the winner is known as 'first past the post'.

The majority of people think this is the best system. It is straightforward and easy to understand. Each elector has one vote in one constituency. It also tends to produce decisive results in elections.

Other people argue that the present system is unfair, because the proportion of MPs that a party gets may not equal the proportion of support that the party has in the country as a whole. For example, in the 2001 general election the Labour Party won 40% of the vote, but gained 62% of the MPS. They argue that between 2001 and 2005 the Labour Party was over-represented in the House of Commons.

Instead of the first past the post system, some people want a system of proportional representation (PR) introduced. A form of PR is used for the Scottish Parliament, the Welsh Assembly and the Northern Ireland Assembly. However, when a referendum was held in 2011 on whether to change the system of electing MPs to the Alternative Vote (AV) system, over two-thirds of voters voted against changing the system.

United Kingdom Alternative Vote referendum		
At present, the UK uses the "first past the post" system to elect MPs to the House of Commons. Should the "alternative vote" system be used instead?		
Results		
Yes or no	**Votes**	**Percentage**
✓ Yes	6,152,607	32.1%
✗ No	**13,013,123**	67.9%
Valid votes	19,165,730	99.41%
Invalid or blank votes	113,292	0.59%
Total votes	**19,279,022**	**100.00%**
Voter turnout		42.2%
Electorate		45,684,501

Debating the issue

Organise either a formal debate or a boxing debate* on the motion:

"The house believes that the present system of voting is unfair and that a system of proportional representation should be introduced."

* In a boxing debate, the class is split into two teams – one supporting the motion, one against the motion. Members of each team take it in turns to speak.

Proportional representation

Proportional representation (PR) is an electoral system where the number of votes cast for a party is approximately equal to the number of votes cast for that party. For example, if a party gained 30% of the votes, it would get around 30% of the seats.

Several voting systems have been suggested to replace the system of 'first past the post'.

The alternative vote

Under this system, rather than putting a X next to their preferred candidate, voters would list candidates in their constituency in order of preference. If one candidate receives over 50% of the vote, they are elected. But if no one achieves that, the second choices for the least popular candidate are redistributed. That process is repeated until one candidate gets an absolute majority.

The single transferable vote (STV)

Under this system several MPs would be elected in multi-member constituencies, which would, therefore be larger than the present constituencies. Voters would list candidates in order of preference. A candidate would be elected once they had achieved a certain share of the votes.

The additional member system (AMS)

Under this system, voters have two votes: one for an individual candidate in a single-member constituency and one for a regional member. Individual candidates are elected using the first-past the post system. The regional members are elected according to each party's share of the vote, so that the number of additional members a party gets is proportional to its share of the vote.

Reform of the electoral system

Arguments for change

1 Though voting through PR is quite complicated, it is a fairer system, as it gives voters more power and choice by enabling them to list their preferences.

2 PR gives each party the number of MPs that corresponds to its share of the vote throughout the country.

3 Minority parties, such as the Green Party, stand a better chance of getting MPs into Parliament.

4 PR will stop governments who get less than 50% of the vote from being able to force unpopular laws through Parliament.

5 PR will bring the UK into line with its European partners, most of whom are used to having PR and coalition governments.

6 Constituencies would be larger and represented by several MPs. Voters would be able to contact the MP of their choice.

Arguments against change

1 Voting under the current system is simple and easy to understand.

2 The winning party usually has an overall majority in the House of Commons. This produces strong governments that can stay in power long enough to pass the laws they want.

Different types of business

Businesses vary in size from small businesses owned and run by one person to large national and multinational companies employing tens of thousands of people in many different companies.

Working for yourself

When you work for yourself you are called a 'sole trader'. You work on your own and are responsible for your own business. On the one hand, this can be very risky. If your costs get out of control, you could lose a lot of money. On the other hand, if you make a lot of money you get to keep all of the profit.

It can be difficult to raise the money to start the business. Banks are less keen to lend money to sole traders. This is because of the high rate of failure. Of each three new businesses started each year, two will fail. It is very easy to lose all of your money. This is known as going bankrupt.

If your business goes bankrupt, you are personally responsible for all the money owed to other people. This money is known as debts. You may have to sell your car and even your house if, as a sole trader, your business is bankrupt.

Sole traders are very common in the service industries. Examples include shopkeepers, writers and hairdressers.

Partnerships

In a partnership, you share the risk. Between two and 20 people run the business.

They own it, control it, provide the starting money for it and share the profits from it.

To form a partnership you sign a special agreement called a Deed of Partnership.

Because more than one person is involved, it is easier to raise money for this type of business and to share the work and responsibility. However, if the business fails, all the partners have to pay off the debts.

One advantage of working in a partnership is that different people can provide different skills. For example, Trevor worked on his own as a plumber and his sister Shereen worked as an electrician. They formed a partnership with their friend Amrit, a carpenter, to do household maintenance work. They called themselves Household Solutions.

Azam owns and runs a café.

Working for a company

Working for a company removes a lot of risk. You will be paid a salary by the company, and usually will not receive a share of the profits. This is how many people work in the UK. However, your salary will usually be fixed. This means that even if the company is very successful, you will still receive the same amount of money.

Also, the company may fail. When the retailers Woolworths collapsed in 2008, thousands of people lost their jobs.

WH Smith is a national company selling books, magazines and stationery

Shell is a multi-national company with business interests all over the world

Working in the public, private or voluntary sector

If you own your own company, or work for a private company, this is known as working in the private sector. The rewards in the private sector are large, but the risks are the greatest.

Alternatively, you may work for the Government, for example, as a nurse, doctor or teacher. This is known as working in the public sector. Public sector wages tend to be lower than in the private sector. However, the risks are lower, as the government is always going to need staff for public services, for example, in hospitals and in schools.

A third option is working in the voluntary sector. This can involve working as a volunteer, or as a paid member of staff, for some sort of charity. For example, Tina worked as a nurse until she retired. Now she works as a volunteer for Age Concern, which helps and supports older people.

In groups

On your own, list the advantages and disadvantages of **a)** working for yourself **b)** working for a company. Then share your views in a group discussion.

Discuss what the differences are between working in the private sector and working in the public sector. Which sector provides more job security? Which provides the most rewards? Which is more risky?

How is a firm organised

In order for a business to be successful, it must perform a variety of different tasks. This means that different people play different roles in the business.

Here is an example of a small business that produces goods.

Production

Production makes the goods that are being sold. It tries to do this as cheaply as possible. This ensures that costs are low, so that profits can be high.

Research

Research and development (or R&D) researches new products for sale in the future. For example, a toymaker develops new toys and games. They work with customers to find out what new games they like playing, and what would sell the best.

Public relations

The image of a company can greatly affect its sales. This affects its profits. Public relations ensures that the image of the company is presented in the best possible way. This involves communicating with customers, management and the company workforce, as well as the media.

Sales and marketing

Sales and marketing are responsible for selling as many of the goods as possible. It advertises the goods for sale and sets sales targets to be reached.

Support services

Every company needs cleaners, food for the staff to eat, secretaries, electricity and computers. These are all known as support services.

Finance and accounting

These departments make sure that costs are kept low and revenue (income) is as high as possible.

Management

The group of managers that control the overall management of the company is called the Board of Directors. At the head of this group is the Managing Director of the company.

In pairs

Research a local business to find out how it is organised. It could be a manufacturing firm, a shop or a business that provides a service of some kind. Contact the firm to find out if it has a website you could visit and what leaflets (if any) they produce about the firm. Then arrange to visit the firm to interview someone about how it is organised. Before your visit, make a list of questions about the information you want to obtain. Then, after the visit, draft a report to present to the rest of your class.

Social entrepreneurs

An entrepreneur is a person who creates a new business. Social entrepreneurs try to create new businesses that do not just operate for profit. They also have some sort of social aim. This might be:

- To create more jobs in an area of high unemployment.
- To recycle more local rubbish so it doesn't end up in a landfill.
- To educate young people about the dangers of binge drinking.
- To provide a service missing in the local community (e.g. meals on wheels).
- To provide training opportunities for young people.

A social enterprise

A business with social aims is called a social enterprise. Green Works is a social enterprise that collects unwanted office furniture from big companies like Marks and Spencer and recycles it to sell at a discount.

Green Works charges a fee to take desks, chairs, tables and coat-stands etc to one of its six London warehouses. These are sold to schools, colleges, charities, housing associations and small businesses.

"I'm here to stop furniture filling up landfill, not to boost profits so that I can holiday in Barbados," says the founder Colin Crooks.

Since 2000, his business has taken more than 60,000 tonnes of furniture that would have ended up in landfill.

To carry out its work, Green Works employs and trains marginalised groups, including homeless people and ex-offenders. It has created over 800 training and employment places over the last 10 years. Sending the furniture to landfill would only employ two people.

In groups

Use the internet to find out about existing social enterprise businesses. What kind of social enterprise would benefit your local community? Imagine that a local person has offered to fund the setting up of a business that would benefit the community. Share your ideas for a social enterprise and choose one of them to present to the rest of the class. Then, as a class, vote to decide which group has the best proposal.

For your file

Write a statement saying why you agree or disagree with the social enterprise that the class chose as the best proposal.

Financing a business

Businesses need money for a variety of reasons. Firstly, they need money to buy the raw materials it takes to make the goods they manufacture. They will also need money to rent or buy premises, for example for a factory and for the machinery required to make the goods. These are known as fixed costs.

Secondly, the business will also need to pay wages for its workers who make the goods. These are known as the workforce. Heating, lighting and electricity will also need to be paid for. The factory will need cleaning, which also costs money. The goods will need promoting through sales and marketing. All of these are known as variable costs.

Finally, a firm may need money to pay off a bank loan that was taken out to start up the business, or to pay shareholders a percentage of the profits.

The money-go-round

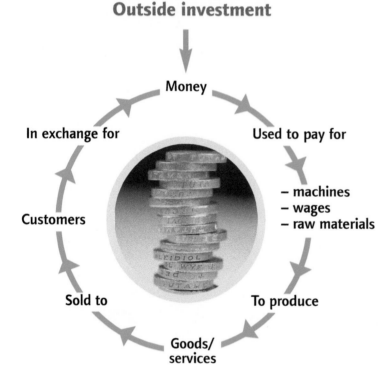

Outside investment

Money

In exchange for — Used to pay for

Customers

Sold to

Goods/services

To produce

— machines
— wages
— raw materials

In groups

You are partners in a small manufacturing business that is doing well. You need to raise money to buy more equipment and to take on more staff. Discuss how you could raise the money. Which of the four options would you choose? Give reasons for your views.

Four ways of raising money

1 The first way of raising money is to put your own money into the business. This is easy to do, but very risky. If your business fails, you will lose all of your money.

2 A second way of raising money is to borrow the money from a bank. This is known as a loan. However, you have to pay more money back than you borrowed. The extra amount you pay is known as interest.

3 A third way is to invite several people to help run your business. Each of these people is known as a partner. The partners each put an amount of their money into the business, so they end up sharing the risk. But if the business is a success they also share the profits.

4 Finally, you can sell parts of your business in order to raise money. This is done by dividing your business into shares. For example, if you had 100 shares in your business, each person who owned one share would own 1% of the business. These people are known as shareholders.

In return for investing money, shareholders expect a share of the profits. This is known as a dividend. If the value of the business goes up, shareholders can sell their shares for more money as well.

Risk and profit

Just because you have raised the money, it doesn't mean that the business will be a success. Unexpected things can happen. Prices can rise, demand can fall (when people don't want your goods or services so much), competitors can take away your share of the market or illness can hit the employees of the company, creating extra costs.

Jonathan's story

Jonathan runs a transport business, moving goods from one place to another. In 2008, he had ten lorries and was making a healthy profit. He employed 20 people and was planning to expand the business further.

But the recession meant that several of his customers went bankrupt, some owing Jonathan money. At the same time, the cost of fuel soared. A major part of Jonathan's running costs is diesel. Instead of being able to expand the business, Jonathan found that he could no longer afford to run ten lorries.

He was faced with having to put up his prices to cover his costs and he lost some of his customers. Reluctantly, he decided to reduce the number of lorries he had and to make several of his staff redundant.

He now has only four lorries and is struggling to make a profit.

In groups

Imagine you are running a factory in the UK. Your profits have been hit by a global recession. This means the world economy is shrinking, and demand for your goods is falling. You need to do something, otherwise you will go out of business.

Study these four options and decide what you would do:

1 Negotiate with your suppliers to pay less for your raw materials. This will reduce your costs. But it also means that the workers who produce the raw materials in developing countries, who are already poorly paid, may have their wages cut.

2 Cut the amount of goods you are producing. This will means jobs will have to be cut and unemployment in the local area will rise.

3 Cut the price of your goods. This means that you will make less profit and you will have to cut the wages of your workforce too.

4 Try to sell the business to prevent yourself going bankrupt. But it may be hard to find a buyer, so you may have to reduce the price and sell the business for much less than you think it is worth.

For your file

"I'll do whatever I can to save my business, even if there are knock-on effects from any action I take to do so. It's not my fault there's a global recession and that unemployment will rise if I have to cut my workforce. After all, you've got to put yourself and your family first."

Say what you think of this point of view.

The school environment

"It doesn't matter what the school looks like, it's only a school."

"The appearance of the school and grounds is important. They create the atmosphere of the school."

"It's up to everyone to look after the school and make sure the environment is pleasant."

"It's up to the local council to look after the school."

"People put up with things about the school environment that they'd never put up with in their own homes."

"Schools are like all public places. The environment suffers because people don't see it as their responsibility."

In groups

Discuss these comments about the school environment. How much do you think the school environment matters? Why do people put up with things at school that they wouldn't put up with at home? Whose responsibility is it to look after the school environment?

An environmental survey

Carry out a survey of the condition of the school's buildings and grounds. Draw up a chart like the one below and rate the condition of each area as either good, fair or bad.

Area	Condition		
	Good	Fair	Bad
School gates/signs	☐	☐	☐
School drives/pathways	☐	☐	☐
School grounds/yards	☐	☐	☐
Playing fields	☐	☐	☐
Entrance hall	☐	☐	☐
Corridors	☐	☐	☐
Staircases	☐	☐	☐
Noticeboards	☐	☐	☐
Assembly hall	☐	☐	☐
Dining room	☐	☐	☐
Science labs	☐	☐	☐
Technology rooms	☐	☐	☐
Art room	☐	☐	☐
Music block	☐	☐	☐
Gymnasium	☐	☐	☐
Toilets	☐	☐	☐
General classrooms	☐	☐	☐

In groups

1 Show each other your surveys and discuss your views of the condition of the different areas of the school. Choose three areas as priorities for improvement and share your ideas in a class discussion.

2 Imagine that it has been announced that schools can bid for up to £50,000 of lottery money for projects to improve the school environment. Discuss ideas for projects to improve your school environment. Choose one and draft a proposal to put to the rest of the class. Debate the various proposals, then vote to choose what your class's project would be.

3 Talk about what you could do to improve the appearance and atmosphere of your tutor group room. Organise a working party to investigate what any suggested improvements might cost and, if necessary, approach the appropriate school committee to apply for funds or hold a fundraising event. Then carry out the improvements.

The local environment

Eco-Schools

The Eco-Schools programme is an international initiative designed to encourage whole-school action for the environment

The aims of the Eco-Schools programme are:

- To improve the school environment.
- To reduce litter and waste.
- To reduce energy and water use.
- To devise efficient ways of travelling to and from school.
- To build strong partnerships with community groups.

Case study: Royal Manor College, Dorset

Since becoming an eco-school, the school has taken action to improve the environment and to follow a sustainable development programme. The achievements of the student-led eco-group include:

Students building a greenhouse from plastic bottles as part of a recycling project.

- Persuading a local company to supply and install a solar voltaic panel and boiler on the science department, which provides hot water for the science department.
- Creating a wildlife pond, which is used as part of the science curriculum.
- Creating an allotment area, which grows vegetables for distribution to older people in the local community.
- Creating a composting area for green waste.
- Ensuring that all classrooms have paper recycling bins.
- Organising print cartridge recycling.
- Introducing an anti-litter campaign.
- Drawing up a transport plan to encourage students to travel on foot, by bicycle or public transport rather than go to school by car.

From 'Leading Sustainable Schools'

What is sustainable development?

Sustainable development means meeting our present needs without compromising the ability of future generations to meet their needs. It means making progress and improving the quality of our life without destroying the planet or having a bad effect on other people in the process.

To have a sustainable lifestyle we have to consider the resources we use, whether we are producing too much waste, how much pollution we produce, and how we affect the natural environment.

Everyone can get involved. You can start by doing small things like switching off the light when you leave a room and making sure you recycle cans and paper.

In groups

On your own, make a list of things you can do individually to help save energy, cut down on waste and reduce pollution. Then compare your lists in a group discussion.

For your file

Use the internet to research the Eco-Schools programme and what it has achieved. Write a statement describing its achievements and arguing that every school should become an eco-school.

Making a difference — changing places

Young people throughout the UK are making a difference to the environment by getting involved in projects organised by their schools, local councils and organisations such as the environmental charity Groundwork.

These charities support communities in need, working with partners to help improve the quality of people's lives, their prospects and potential and the places where they live, work and play. Their vision is of a society of sustainable communities that are vibrant, healthy and safe, which respect the local and global environment and where individuals and enterprise prosper.

GROUNDWORK

CHANGING PLACES
CHANGING LIVES

Derelict land transformed into community garden

Young people in the North Prospect area of Plymouth took part in a Groundwork project that transformed a piece of derelict land in Woodhey Road into a community garden. The land was a much-used shortcut between Ham and North Prospect and attracted anti-social behaviour as well as litter.

"Before the project it was really horrible," says Emma, who was a young volunteer on the project. "There was no way anyone could play safely there as it was full of syringes and broken glass. Because we had nowhere else to

go we used to hang around on the street, but that got too dangerous as there was a lot of anti-social behaviour locally.

"The project has made such a big difference. The garden is a place people can go either just to sit or to play. There are trees, a willow tunnel, a sand pit and a gazebo. It attracts so many people and there's a lot less anti-social behaviour."

The project has taught the community that by working together we can achieve amazing results and make a difference to the areas we live in.

In groups

Investigate your local environment to identify what you think might be done to improve it. Use your IT skills to design a questionnaire that surveys people's opinions, to analyse the results and to draft a proposal. Either send a copy of your proposal to the local newspaper or invite a local councillor to come to the school to discuss your ideas.

Tidy Towns

Tidy Towns is an initiative between Keep Wales Tidy, local councils and the Welsh government. Volunteers 'adopt' a local area that needs attention. Communities are encouraged to focus on cleaning up waste black-spots.

Projects undertaken by groups include:

- **Litter picks and clean-ups**
- **Path maintenance**
- **Dune management**
- **Installing benches**
- **Creating picnic sites**
- **Invasive species clearance and management**
- **Improving disabled access**
- **Developing community gardens and allotments**
- **Running waste amenities**
- **Habitat management and biodiversity**
- **Churchyard improvements**

School wins top environmental award

Pupils from a North Wales school who undertook the task of restoring an ancient woodland to its former glory have been given a top environmental award by Keep Wales Tidy.

Pupils at Holywell High School in Flintshire were so disgusted with the state of the woodland that borders their school that they decided to mount a major restoration programme.

After a massive litter clearance, they cleared glades to encourage the growth of bluebells, created paths and prepared way-markers.

Go MADD
Organise a Make A Difference Day

Make a Difference Day (MADD) is an annual event, usually a Saturday in October. Thousands of people throughout the UK donate a few hours of their time to help the local community in some way, for example by cleaning graffiti off a bus shelter, cleaning up the local pond or doing some shopping for an older person.

In groups

Organise your own MADD event to take place for two to three hours one evening after school or on a Saturday morning.

First, make a list of the different things you could do to help the local community in the time available. Share your ideas in a class discussion. Draw up a class list of jobs and get people to volunteer for them. Appoint a committee of four or five people to act as a steering group to plan the event and to make sure that everyone involved knows what is expected of them.

After the event, discuss how it went and talk about what went well and what you would do differently when organising a similar event in the future.

For your file

Write a press release to send to your local paper explaining how you organised your Make a Difference Day and what people did.

Attitudes towards older people

Ageism

To be old in Britain today is considered by some to be 'past it', 'over the hill' or a 'has-been'.

Such attitudes towards older people are widespread in a society such as ours, which values youth, beauty and material possessions.

For many people, who are not old themselves, growing old is something to be feared. It is seen as a time of loss and withdrawal from life, rather than as a natural development that occurs gradually over time. Yet if you were to ask older people how they feel about their age, they are likely to respond by saying that although they may look old, they still feel young inside.

Many of the negative images we have about older people are perpetuated by the media, which tends to portray them as victims of crime, poverty or neglect, or as figures of fun. To judge a person negatively simply because they are old is ageist.

Once you become aware of it, however, ageism is apparent in all areas of life – from the derogatory way we refer to older people as 'geriatrics' or 'old fogies' to the patronising way we treat older people as if they are children and need protecting. It also shows itself in the embarrassment and condemnation we express if an older person continues to have an interest in sex or if they prefer to dress in a style we think is inappropriate for their age.

Ageism is at the root of some common assumptions we make about older people – that they are all stubborn and inflexible, dependent and institutionalised, senile and sexless.

Old age and memory loss

Many people who live to be very old become forgetful. For example, they may call people by their wrong name. This is considered to be a normal part of the ageing process.

Most older people retain their full mental powers until the end of their lives. However, some older people – between 10 and 20 per cent – suffer from varying degrees of dementia.

A person who suffers from dementia gets muddled and confused because they cannot remember things. They may forget where they put their possessions, lose track of the time or the day of the week, and confuse objects, for example, mistaking the washing machine for the fridge. A person with severe dementia may be unable to recognise people or places.

There is no single known cause of dementia. Scientists are carrying out research to try to understand dementia, but, until it is fully understood, in many cases it cannot be treated.

In groups

Study the article on ageism (left). Discuss how people regard the elderly and the way that they are presented by the media. Do you think society is ageist? Appoint a spokesperson and share your views in a class discussion.

Do you think that people undervalue the contribution that older people can make to society? Talk about older people that you know and about how they spend their time.

For your file

Write an article about the causes and effects of ageism. You could interview a number of older people and include their views in your article.

The problems faced by older people

Survey finds 'two worlds of old age'

A survey of older people's lifestyles found that one in four people aged 80 and over worries about being able to afford food, while two-thirds are concerned about paying for clothing or heating bills.

The findings are from a survey of 1,317 readers, aged 55 to over 90, of *Yours*, a magazine for older people.

While the majority, 90%, enjoyed retirement, a small but significant group faced a bleak old age.

The research provided evidence of 'two worlds of old age,' said the report's author, Alisoun Milne.

"If you live in your own home, in a shared household, with an occupational pension and are in the early stages of retirement, up to 75, you tend to be OK. But if you don't have that financial backing, live on your own, and are 80 or older, that tends not to be the case."

Over half of those surveyed said they were unable to afford holidays, nearly 40% could barely buy presents, and a quarter found that paying for household maintenance, heating and clothing could be problematic.

"Most older people enjoy retirement and contribute a great deal to their families and communities," said Tessa Harding of Help the Aged. "But the dire poverty of some is a real tragedy in a wealthy society."

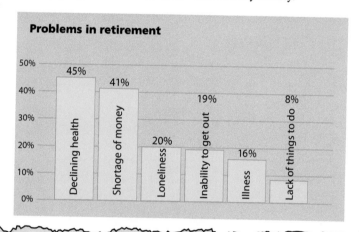

Problems in retirement

Declining health	45%
Shortage of money	41%
Loneliness	20%
Inability to get out	19%
Illness	16%
Lack of things to do	8%

Study the article and graph and discuss what you learn from them about the problems some older people face in old age.

Caring for older people

Many frail older people are only able to continue living in the community because they receive support from their carers and from services provided by the community, such as visiting care assistants, day care and respite care.

Older people who are frail or very disabled often cannot go out unless transport is provided for them, so transport is provided for them in special vehicles.

Once they become too frail or ill to be able to cope in their own homes, many older people have to be cared for in residential or nursing homes.

Social services departments spend an average of 64% of their budget for older people on supporting residents in residential and nursing homes. However, there are limited financial resources and older people can spend a lot of time in hospital before admission to residential or nursing care.

What role should the family play?

'Out of 1000 adults, 57% agreed that there was some obligation to care for older people in the family, 37% did not agree.' What role do you think the family should play in looking after older people?

What can the problems be when older people
a) live with the family;
b) live in their own homes?

What other alternatives are there?

What can be done to support older people who live on their own and have no relatives?

An ageing population – society in the 21st century

Forecasts for the future

- As the 21st century progresses there will be fewer younger people and more older people:

- Between 1995 and 2040, the number of children under the age of 10 will drop by nearly 20% – in the same period the number of people aged 65 will increase by over 60%.

- In 1961 there were almost four people of working age to support each pensioner; by 2040 there will be only two.

- In 1951 there were 33 centenarians; in 2031 there will be 36,000.

- By 2040 there will be an extra 20 dependent pensioners for every 100 people of working age.

- Admissions of older people to hospital are increasing by 4% a year, and over the next 35 years the proportion of people over 65 will rise by 30%.

- The population of pensionable age will rise to 12 million by 2021, and will peak at nearly 15.5 million around 2038.

In groups

Study the statistics in the article (below) and discuss how the age profile of society is changing.

How will life be different in the 21st century?

- People born in the 1990s will be over 50 by the middle of the century. If you will be 50 or more in the year 2040 then the changes in society will affect you.

- When the National Health Service was designed, life expectancy was around 50 years. Today it is 80 years.

- By 2016 there will be almost 24 million households in Britain (23% more than in 1991) and more than one in three will consist of people living on their own.

- Since 2010, 52% of workers do some work at home. 8% of workers will be working 30 hours per week at home.

- How do you think life will change because of these things?

- In the 21st century, Britain will need 5 million extra homes. Do you think we should expand into the countryside

There are unlikely to be major problems in the short to medium-term future of health and care, but significant challenges could face society after 2020. Medical advances in the 21st century will mean more and more conditions can be treated. But treatment costs money. The need to ration or control health service expenditure is increasingly being debated, and there are serious risks that the needs of older people will be seen as an unacceptable cost.

to build the extra homes needed for the future?

- Your retirement could last longer than your schooldays. Which do you agree with – individuals should be able to choose at what age they stop working, or retirement should be compulsory in order to allow younger people to have jobs?

- By 2040 there will be only two working people to support every pensioner (as opposed to four working people in 1961). Will there be pensions for people (which means YOU) in the future? Without pensions, how would old people manage?

In groups

1 What does rationing mean? How can people be given a fixed allowance of medical treatment? Would that be a fair system?

2 Should people expect medical treatment if **a)** they don't have a healthy lifestyle, **b)** they take part in dangerous sports, or **c)** they travel to countries where there are health risks?

3 Do you think people would be prepared to pay more taxes to get whatever treatment they need?

4 Can you think of a system that is fair to everyone, whatever their age?

In groups

Thinking ahead

Study the stories on this page and discuss the questions and implications.

Liz's story

17 years old in the year 2010. "I'm training to be a computer programmer. I'll learn new skills as I go along, that way I've got a better chance of being employed."

Q How can Liz help herself to stay employed?

47 years old in the year 2040. "I've started volunteering a few hours a week when I have a spell without work. They said I'd enjoy it and I can't believe how much I get out of it."

Q Do we value Liz's volunteer work?

87 years old in the year 2080, still healthy. "I'm perfectly fit enough to work and I can't imagine giving it up. I do voluntary work. I'm helping myself and others at the same time."

Q Why should Liz retire if she doesn't want to?

Patrick's story

17 years old in the year 2010, a shop assistant. "I've just had my eyes corrected with laser surgery. No more glasses for me. It's done my confidence the world of good."

Q Should Patrick get whatever healthcare he needs throughout his life?

47 years old in the year 2040, a manager. "I had a small stroke this year and I've lost the use of my right arm. Magazines are always going on about eating healthy foods and taking exercise, but I never took any notice. Now I wish I had."

Q Is it Patrick's responsibility to stay well with a healthy lifestyle?

87 years old in the year 2080. "My daughter's got a life of her own and I don't want to depend on her. I'm lucky I've got someone to come in and help a few hours each day. My community pays her wages. I don't know what I'd do without them, but the government can't pay for everyone."

Q Who will Patrick want to look after him when he can't take care of himself?

For your file

Write about the changes that you think you will see during your lifetime as a result of the changing age profile of society. What, if anything, do you think you need to do to prepare for them?

The foods you eat

Spoilt for choice

Walk down any supermarket aisle and you would be hard pushed to realise that 800 million people in the world do not have enough food to meet their basic nutritional needs. The shelves groan with goodies, from the bare essentials such as sugar and bread to exotic foods like starfruit and ostrich steaks. However, having a choice comes at a price:

- Producers often struggle to make a living as supermarkets squeeze them for rock-bottom prices for their goods.

- Consumers are often offered food that has been sprayed with pesticides. Nearly all fruit and vegetables have been grown using pesticides. An apple might have received 35 pesticide treatments by the time it reaches the supermarket.

- Foods often come from animals that have been treated with antibiotics. Animals reared in intensive factory farms are more likely to become ill, so they are regularly dosed with antibiotics. There is evidence that eating this meat leads to resistance to antibiotics in humans.

- The environment suffers because foods are air-freighted vast distances, so that we can have foods such as strawberries all the year round. In addition to airline and road freight emissions, the foods are wrapped in packaging that may be non-biodegradable.

Organic food

Any food labelled organic must be grown or reared without the use of pesticides, artificial fertilisers, genetic modification and antibiotics. Weeds and pests are controlled by natural techniques and animals are reared in humane conditions.

Organic food is usually more expensive than mass-produced food, which is a reflection of the extra costs of its production. Despite the cost, an increasing number of people are converting to organic food because they believe it is better for animals and the environment and is both healthier and tastes better.

Genetically Modified (GM) foods

Genetic engineering allows scientists to create new breeds in the laboratory. It is done by altering the genes, the vital blueprints inside all living cells that give plants and animals their different characteristics. Most GM crops, however, are engineered to be resistant to pesticides, so that when they are sprayed on a field, everything but the crop will die.

The health effects of eating GM foods are as yet unknown, with the scientific community divided over possible risks to human health. There are also concerns that GM crops will cause genetic pollution by releasing pollen into the environment and transferring their genetic qualities to wild plants.

Synthetic burgers – the food of the future?

The world's first stem cell burger was cooked and eaten in London in 2013. It was grown in a laboratory in an experiment which could lead to artificial meat in supermarkets within 10 years. The meal has been made from 3,000 strips of artificial beef, each the size of a grain of rice.

Scientists are hoping the development will meet the growing worldwide demand for beef, lamb, pork and chicken. Professor Mark Post, the Dutch scientist who developed the burger, said that synthetic meat would need 99% less land than livestock, between 82 and 98 per cent less water and would produce between 78 per cent and 95 per cent less greenhouse gas.

The Food Standards Agency said that the burger must undergo a stringent safety assessment before it could go on the market.

In groups

1 Discuss what you learn from the information in this article about:
a) where our food comes from, **b)** how it is produced, and **c)** the effects that producing, packaging and transporting foods to stock our supermarket shelves have on the environment.

2 Discuss what is meant by 'organic foods'. Why are they considered by many people to be healthier than other foods? Do you think it is worth paying the extra price for organic foods?

3 What are the arguments for and against genetically modified foods? Do you think we should continue to develop them, or is the possibility that they will damage the environment too great a risk to take?

4 What are your views on synthetic meat? Would you be prepared to eat an artificial burger?

5 What are your views on factory farming? Do you try to avoid eating foods that have been produced by factory farming? Is factory farming 'cruel and unnecessary'?

For your file

Write a submission to a newspaper expressing your views on one or more of the issues about the foods we eat that are raised in this article.

World hunger

Many people in the world do not get enough nourishment from the food they eat. **Malnutrition** is the term used to describe lack of nutrition in a person's diet. It is estimated that almost 750 million people suffer from malnutrition – more than twice the whole population of Europe.

> "Throughout Africa food shortages are common, although more food than ever is being produced in the world. The problem is that some countries and people have more than they need while others do not have enough."
> Christian Aid

Why
do famines happen?

Famine is a crisis in which starvation from too little food results in a sharp increase in deaths.

Hunger and malnutrition are more common than famine. One in five people doesn't get enough of the right kind of food to lead fully productive lives – they are vulnerable to disease, infection and parasites and grow up with weak bones and muscles. Malnutrition contributes to short life expectancy and is especially dangerous for children, affecting their strength and their ability to grow, to learn and to perform complex tasks.

Poverty

Poverty is the main cause of famine. People who live in poverty are always more vulnerable to natural disasters. When floods and droughts occur in wealthy countries, people don't starve because they don't rely on their land for food – they often have a salary, savings, insurance and, as a last resort the government has enough money and food to get emergency supplies through. But when you have little and lose that – be it your crop or your house – there is nothing left to fall back on.

International trade

Food security is also affected by both local conditions and government policies. Many people argue that international trade policies are unfair and penalise poorer countries, many of which are caught in a debt trap which hits the poorest hardest. In Zambia almost half the population is under-nourished. Yet still it bears one of the heaviest debt burdens in the world. For every man, woman and child, the Zambian government owes £437 to creditors.

War

War diverts valuable resources away from development. In a war-zone families cannot successfully plant or tend crops, they have difficulty storing food for times of hardship, markets often close and the warring parties can prevent help reaching people. They can be forced to leave their homes and to become refugees, relying for their survival on food aid.

In groups

Study the information on these pages. Discuss the reasons people give for why there is hunger in Sub-Saharan Africa. Which are true? What are the real reasons why there is hunger in those countries?

For your file

Write a statement saying what you have learned from these pages about the reasons for hunger and malnutrition in some parts of the world and about how the problem could be solved.

Unequal shares

According to the United Nations the average person should eat no less than 2,400 calories a day. If a person's calorie intake is constantly below that level, they are likely to suffer from malnutrition.

Most of the people who suffer from malnutrition live in the poor countries in the developing world. The world produces enough grain to provide every person with 3,000 calories a day. And that doesn't include all the beans, fruit and vegetables that are grown. The problem is that the world's food is not distributed equally.

While millions of people do not get enough to eat, people in Western Europe, North America and Japan on average eat over 25% more calories than they need. In poorer countries, the richest 10% of the population eat more than twice the number of calories eaten by the poorest 20%.

Why are they hungry?

Half the people of Sub-Saharan Africa don't have enough to eat. Here are some reasons people give.

- *People in Africa are lazy.*
- *There is not enough food in the world.*
- *African people have too many children.*
- *Some people in the world get more than their fair share of food.*
- *Farmers in Africa need more pesticides and fertilisers.*
- *African farmers are not given a fair deal in the world market.*
- *Drought and famine are natural disasters which cannot be prevented.*
- *Farmers don't have enough good land on which to grow food.*

Ten ways to beat world hunger

1 Increase the amount of aid to small farmers to help them stay on their land, for example, by giving them seeds and tools as well as food.

2 Cut down the amount of food that rich countries import from developing countries.

3 Reduce the amount of land used for growing cash crops.

4 Train farmers in methods that will increase the yield from their land.

5 Educate people so that they know which foods to grow and eat for a healthy diet.

6 Send more food aid to poor countries.

7 Introduce land reforms so that the land in developing countries is distributed more fairly.

8 Get more people in rich countries to change their eating habits, for example, by becoming vegetarians.

9 Cancel the debts that the governments of Third World countries owe to western banks.

10 Repair environmental damage and improve the quality of the land, for example, by tree-planting projects.

In groups

Discuss the ten suggestions for helping to solve the problem of world hunger. Which do you agree with? Which do you disagree with? Put a selection of 5 suggestions in order of importance starting with the one you think will have the most long-term effect. Can you suggest other ways to help?

Water – a vital resource

A person needs about 5 litres of water a day for cooking and drinking.

But to stay clean and healthy a further 25–45 litres are needed per person.

The water crisis

Water is vital for all living things to survive – a few days without it and people die. In a rich country like the UK everyone has access to water. Yet for 80 countries – with 40 per cent of the world's population – lack of water is a constant threat.

Lack of water in many places in the world is an ever-worsening crisis. There is not enough water to drink and to keep crops and farm animals alive. Increases in population mean there is less water available for each person. Climate change, caused by pollution of the atmosphere, is making some countries that are already short of water even hotter and drier. Demand for water is doubling every 20 years.

The fresh clean water that is available is often wasted and misused. When people are poor they have no money to pump and pipe water. They cannot even afford proper houses. There are no sewage works to dispose of waste. As a result, what clean water there is gets mixed with dirty water and germs breed, causing illnesses. The United Nations estimates that

dirty water causes 80% of disease in developing countries and kills 3.4 million people annually. The UN believes that the lack of clean water is becoming a terrible crisis for the world. Nations may go to war to fight to control the supply of water, as they have done in the past to fight for oil.

There are ways of solving the problem. The charity Water Aid starts at the beginning, with the poor people who need the water most. These people have no access to expensive technology so all schemes are kept simple. Wells are dug and maintained with hand tools. Hand pumps can be provided so that whole villages can be supplied with clean water. Water can be brought in by pipeline and gravity does the rest.

Just as importantly, simple sewage schemes are organised so that dirty water is kept away from the clean. Many hours of work in carrying water is avoided, children stay healthy, and a huge problem gets smaller.

How much do you know about water?

Do this test-yourself quiz, then check the answers (see page 110).

1 How much of our bodies is made up of water?
a. 10% **b.** 70% **c.** 25%

2 What percentage of the world's population does not have access to safe, clean water?
a. 10% **b.** 25% **c.** 70%

3 How much water does it take to flush the toilet?
a. 2·5 litres **b.** 9·5 litres **c.** 19 litres

4 How much water on average does someone in the UK use every day for drinking, washing and cooking?
a. 150 litres **b.** 50 litres **c.** 15 litres

5 Which of these diseases are caused by a lack of safe, clean water and poor sanitation?
a. dysentery **b.** diarrhoea **c.** cholera

6 How many people will die every minute in developing countries from diseases caused by unsafe water?
a. 7 **b.** 1 **c.** 15

7 Traditionally women in Africa and Asia collect the water for the whole family, carrying it up to several miles on their heads or their backs. What is the average weight of the water they carry?
a. 4 kg **b.** 20 kg **c.** 80 kg

8 How much money will provide someone in developing countries with safe water for life?
a. £5 **b.** £15 **c.** £50

From *Water Works*, CAFOD

Millions of people still lack safe water

Nearly 800 million people still don't have clean safe water and 2.5 billion live without toilets.

Every 20 seconds a child under five dies in the developing world from a preventable illness caused by unclean water or lack of basic sanitation. Latrines, uncontaminated water supply and simple handwashing can stop these diseases spreading and destroying communities.

Diarrhoea is the biggest killer of children in Sub-Saharan Africa. Only 61% of the population have access to improved water sources compared to 90% in other parts of the developing world.

From a Tearfund press release

Water wars

Most of the world's great rivers flow across continents, often through several countries. Along their banks are many cities and thousands of farmers relying on irrigation to grow crops. Each year the demand for water grows. Governments decide to dam rivers for hydroelectricity schemes or to store water for the dry season. Downstream it means people who relied on that water for their own use are deprived of it.

One of the best examples is the Nile and its tributaries which flow through seven countries. Egypt uses all the water the Nile can produce to irrigate the desert lands. Sudan, which is upstream, has agreed not to take any more. But some of the poorer countries even further inland – Eritrea, Ethiopia and Uganda – all need more water for growing populations but dare not take it.

In groups

Discuss all the ways that we use water in our homes. How would your life be different if you did not have a water supply in your home, but had to walk 4–5 kilometres to fetch your water from a stand-pipe or a well, using containers?

Study the information on these pages and discuss what you learn from them about the problems many people in the world have of getting sufficient clean water. Why is the demand for water likely to lead to international conflicts in the future?

Assessing your progress and achievements

The aim of this unit is to help you to think about what progress you have made and what you have achieved during Year 8. It gives you the chance to discuss your progress with your tutor, to write a statement about your achievements and to look ahead and set yourself targets for what you hope to achieve in Year 9.

Your subjects

Think about the effort you have made in each of your subjects and what your progress and achievements have been.

For your file

Make a list of all the subjects you are studying and use a five-point scale to give yourself grades for effort and progress in each subject:

1 Excellent   2 Good   3 Satisfactory
4 Poor   5 Unsatisfactory.

Then write a brief comment on your work and progress in your subjects. Give reasons for the grades you have given yourself, and evidence to support your views of your progress and achievements in each subject.

Your skills

Think about your progress in the skills that you are learning as a result of the work you do in your different subjects. These are the key skills:

- Communication skills
- Study skills
- Personal and social skills
- Numeracy skills
- Problem-solving skills
- ICT skills.

For your file

Think about your skills and write a short comment on each one, saying how much you think you have improved that skill during the past year – a lot, quite a lot, only a little. Support your statement by referring to something you have done during the year.

Your activities

Think about the activities you do and what you have achieved in both school and out-of-school activities.

In pairs

Each make a list of all the activities you have taken part in this year, both inside and outside school. Include details of events organised by clubs and societies that you belong to, sports activities, drama and musical activities and any school events that you have been involved in.

Show your list to your partner and discuss any events that were particular highlights because of what you achieved in them.

For your file

Write a short statement giving details of your most significant achievements in your activities during the year.

Your attitude and behaviour

Think about what your attitude and behaviour have been like during the year.
- Have your attendance and punctuality been good?
- Has your behaviour been good
  a) in lessons, **b)** around the school?
- Have you kept up-to-date with your work and handed it in on time?
- Have you volunteered for things and played as full a part as you could in the life of the school?

For your file

Write a short comment summing up your attitude and behaviour during Year 8.

Discussing your progress

Arrange a meeting with your tutor. Show them what you have written about your subjects and your skills and discuss your progress and achievements in Year 8. Compare your own views with those that your teachers have made on subject reports or subject review sheets. Together, decide what your strengths and weaknesses are at present.

Talk about the activities in which you have taken part and what you consider to be your significant achievements, and discuss what you wrote about your attitude and behaviour.

During the meeting listen carefully to what your tutor has to say. Add anything to your statements that your tutor thinks you have missed out. Note down any comments they make in which they disagree with your assessment, either because they think you have been too harsh on yourself, or because they think that you have overestimated the amount of progress you have made.

Recording your achievements

Draft a statement as a record of your progress and achievements during Year 8. Include comments on your subjects, your key skills, your activities and your attitude and behaviour.

Before you put your record in your progress file, show it to your tutor. Agree any changes that your tutor thinks you should make, so that your final statement is what you both consider to be an accurate record of your progress and achievements.

Setting targets

Use your meeting with your tutor to set targets for the future. Assessing what has gone well can help you to identify which subjects and skills you need to improve. When you have identified a subject or a skill that you need to improve, you can set yourself a target and draw up an action plan.

Making an action plan

Step 1 Decide which skills and subjects you would most like to try to improve in Year 9. Discuss with your tutor what you would need to do and the things you would need to change in order to improve in that subject or skill.

Step 2 Together with your tutor agree two or three targets which you both think would be realistic for you to set yourself during Year 9.

Step 3 Draw up an action plan for each of your targets. Think carefully about the various things you need to do in order to achieve a particular target and plan how you are going to achieve it step-by-step. Give yourself plenty of time to achieve it and set yourself deadlines by which you plan to achieve each step.

State clearly what your aim is, then list the steps you are going to take in order to achieve your goal. Here is the action plan that Gaby drew up in order to try to improve her work in History:

Aim: To get a higher grade in History in Year 9.

Steps

1. Use more sources when I'm asked to find out about a topic.

2. Go to the library and look for information in books, on the internet.

3. Make better notes that are focused on the question instead of just copying whole paragraphs from the book.

4. Use more evidence to support the points I make in my written work.

5. Do my History homework in plenty of time instead of at the last minute.

6. Ask Miss Wilks if I can see her once a month to keep a check on how I'm doing.

In pairs

Show each other your action plans. Discuss any problems you think you may have in trying to achieve them and what you might do to overcome them.

Index

Answers to quiz on page 106: 1 b, **2** a, **3** b, **4** a, **5** all of them, **6** a, **7** b (the weight of 20 bags of sugar), **8** b.

Acknowledgments

The publishers wish to thank the following for permission to reproduce text. Every effort has been made to trace copyright holders and to obtain their permission for the use of copyright materials. The publishers will gladly receive any information enabling them to rectify any error or omission at the first opportunity.

p8 'Coping with shyness' adapted from *Pain of shyness* © Telegraph Group Limited; p9 'Coping with classroom mistakes' adapted from *Wise Guides: Self Esteem* by Anita Naik, Hodder & Stoughton; p9 'Learning from your mistakes' from *Growing up* ; p10 'Drugs – facts and fictions' adapted from *Wise Guides: Drugs* by Anita Naik, Hodder & Stoughton; p10 'Is cannabis safe?', from *The Score – Facts about Drugs* © Health Education Authority; p12 'Drugs and the law' from *The Score – Facts about Drugs* © Health Education Authority; p13 'How to turn down drugs and stay friends' from *Wise Guides: Drugs* by Anita Naik, Hodder & Stoughton; p14 Extract from *Roots of the Future*, Commission for Racial Equality, Roots of the Future: Ethnic Diversity in the Making of Britain, London, CRE, 1996; p15 'Stereotype' by John Agard from *Mangoes and Bullets*, Pluto Press 1985, reprinted by kind permission of John Agard c/o Caroline Sheldon Literary Agency; p16 'Negative stereotyping' from *Life Files: Racism* by Jagdish Gundara and Roger Hewitt ©Evans Brothers Limited 1999; p16 'Ethnic minorities still shown as stereotypes in films, says study' from a report ©*The Guardian*, 18 March 2011; p17 'The Press' from *Life Files: Racism* by Jagdish Gundara and Roger Hewitt © Evans Brothers Limited 1999; p21 'Facebook Accused of Creating Gambling Addicts' ©*Mail Online,* 15 July 2012; p24 'It's a dog life without any meat' by Geoff Maynard ©*Daily Express* 2014 Northern and Shell Media Publications; p24 'Are we a nation of telly addicts? 1 in 4 watch up to 6 hours of TV a day…' by Nathan Rao ©*Daily Express* 2014 Northern and Shell Media Publications; p24 'Dementia drug gives new hope' by Jo Willey ©*Daily Express* 2014 Northern and Shell Media Publications; p24 'Migrants shun the English language' by Sarah O'Grady ©*Daily Express* 2014 Northern and Shell Media Publications; p24 'Marathon girl's death linked to sports stimulant' by David Pilditch ©*Daily Express* 2014 Northern and Shell Media Publications; p24 'Foreign aid cash 'is wasted'' ©*Daily Express* 2014 Northern and Shell Media Publications; p24 'Britain 'cherry picking the benefits of Europe'' ©Daily Express 2014 Northern and Shell Media Publications; p24 'Tobacco smuggling spivs 'rob taxpayer'' by David Craik ©*Daily Express* 2014 Northern and Shell Media Publications; p26 'Dealing with divorce' is from *Girls Know Best*, compiled by Michelle Roehm © Beyond Words Publishing Inc 1997, Hillsboro, Oregon, USA; p28 'We had to move to a small flat' from *Dealing with Family Break-up* by Kate Haycock, Wayland Publishers, reprinted with permission of Hodder & Stoughton Publishers; p28 'I get the best of both worlds' from *Dealing with Family Break-up* by Kate Haycock, Wayland Publishers, reprinted with permission of Hodder & Stoughton Publishers; p28 'I want to be with my mates' from *Caught in the Middle* by Alys Swan-Jackson, Piccadilly Press; p29 quotes from Janet, Jason and Rachel from *Caught in the Middle* by Alys Swan-Jackson, Piccadilly Press; p29 'How to cope with step-parents' is from 'Coping with step-families' from *Shout* issue 118 © D.C. Thomson & Co. Ltd; p32 'What is child abuse?' from *Speaking out about Abuse – What Every Young Person Should Know* ©NSPCC, London; p33 'What happens next?' from *Speaking out about Abuse – What Every Young Person Should Know* ©NSPCC, London; p33 'I feel so guilty and ashamed' is from *Sussed and Streetwise* by Jane Goldman, reprinted with permission of Piccadilly Press; p34 'Staying safe in the street' and 'Safety on buses' from *Respect – Your Life Your Choice*, National Children's Safety Books, used with permission of The Access Partnership, Stockport; p35 'Safety in public places' from *Stand Up for Yourself* by Helen Benedict, Hodder & Stoughton; p35 'If someone talks to you persistently' from *Stand Up for Yourself* by Helen Benedict, Hodder & Stoughton; p35 'The golden rule of self-defence' from *Stand Up for Yourself* by Helen Benedict, Hodder & Stoughton; p36 'Staying Safe in Chatrooms' from *Keeping safe online* Cheshire East government website © CEOP/the National Crime Agency/the Crown; p37 'sexting' from thinkuknow.co.uk © CEOP/the National Crime Agency/the Crown; p38 'Police duties and police powers' from *Young Citizen's Passport – Your Guide to the Law*, Hodder & Stoughton; p39 'Helping the police' from *Young Citizen's Passport – Your Guide to the Law*, Hodder & Stoughton; p39 'Reprimands, warnings and prosecutions'

from the leaflet *Youth Justice*; p41 'Doing a good job?' from *Teen Law*, published by Quest, A Young Enterprise company, Queen Elizabeth Boys School, used with permission; p46 'The secret of making friends' from *Friends and Enemies* by Anita Naik, Hodder & Stoughton; p47 'Growing Apart' from *Shout* Summer Special 1999 © D.C. Thomson & Co. Ltd; p46 'The Rules of Friendship' from *Play Stay Keep Safe*, National Children's Safety Books, used with permission of The Access Partnership, Stockport; p48 'How much are you influenced by your friends?' adapted from *Exploring Healthy Sexuality* by Cathy Jewitt, Family Planning Association; p49 'Gangs – know the facts' from *Shout* issue 105, © D.C. Thomson & Co. Ltd; p50 'Is advertising good or bad?' from *Third Stages* by Jim Sweetman © HarperCollins *Publishers*; p51 'China bans adverts for extravagance'© *Daily Telegraph*, 6 February 2013; p52 'The commercial break' from *Third Stages* by Jim Sweetman © HarperCollins *Publishers*; p53 'Advertising and children' from Appendix 3 of 'the Radio Authority's Advertising and Sponsorship Code', March 1997 reprinted with the kind permission of the Radio Authority; p56 'Getting a piece of the action' from Samantha Graham; p62 'What's all the fuss about?' adapted from *Drugs – Reference Point Series* by Anita Ganeri, Scholastic Limited; p64 'Kerry's story' from *Shout* issue 116 © D.C. Thomson & Co. Ltd; p65 'Valerie's story' adapted from *Stolen childhood* by Anita Chaudhuri, 19 October 1991; p65 'Living with someone who drinks – how to cope' from *Wise Guides: Drugs* by Anita Naik, Hodder & Stoughton; p69 'The Henry Box School – school uniform', the Henry Box School; p73 'Dentists warn of piercing perils' adapted from the article 'Dentists warn of illnesses linked to tongue piercing', *The Daily Telegraph*, 21 July 1999 © Telegraph Group Limited; p73 'Sickening sight!' from the letters pages of T2, *The Daily Telegraph*, 12 June 1999 © Telegraph Group Limited; p73 'Should body piercing be banned?' adapted from an article in T2, *The Daily Telegraph*, 5 June 1999 © Telegraph Group Limited; p73 Zoe Rockcliffe's quote from 'A piercing cry of anger' from *The Guardian*, 25 February 1998 © the Guardian; p76 'Sex and Contraception… Your questions answered' adapted from '50 Sex Questions Answered' © *Mizz* 1997; p76 'I'm worried about protection' is from 'Your top 50 problems solved' by Tricia Keitman © *Mizz* 1997; p77 'The rhythm method' from *Wise Guides: Sex* by Anita Naik, Hodder & Stoughton; p77 'Withdrawal' from *Wise Guides: Sex* by Anita Naik, Hodder & Stoughton; p79 'Sex myths' from *Wise Guides: Sex* by Anita Naik, Hodder & Stoughton; p78 'Sexual rights and responsibilities' adapted from *Stand Up for Yourself* by Helen Benedict, Hodder & Stoughton; p79 'What is acceptable in a sexual relationship?' adapted from *Exploring Healthy Sexuality* by Carey Jewitt, 'Family Planning Association', used with permission; p86 'Is the present voting system fair?' adapted from *Democracy in action* by Simon Foster ©HarperCollins*Publishers*; p96 Extracts adapted from text provided by Groundwork, used with permission; p96 'Derelict Land Transformed Into Community Garden' adapted from *North Prospect Community News*, Plymouth City Council ; p98 'Ageism' adapted from information supplied by Help the Aged; p99 'Survey finds two worlds of old age' and the graph 'Problems in retirement' adapted from 'Half over 80s exist on £80 a week or less' by Sarah Hall *The Guardian*, 5 Oct 1999 © The Guardian; p100 'An ageing population' from *Future Forecasts – Statistics Book and Thinking Ahead* – Assembly Book in the Debate of Age Series coordinated by Age Concern, used with permission; p102 'The foods you eat' from 'Spoilt for choice' by John Crace, Guardian Education, 1 February 2000 © The Guardian; p103 'Synthetic burgers – The food of the future?' adapted from *The Daily Telegraph* 28 July 013; p104 'Why do famines happen?' adapted from an article in *Global Express* Edition 11 © 2007 Development Education Project; p105 'Unequal shares' from *Fighting Famine, Beating Hunger* produced by Christian Aid, reprinted with permission; p106 'The Water Crisis' reprinted with permission from 'Water, water everywhere but not a drop to drink' by Paul Brown, *Guardian Education*, 18 March 1997 © The Guardian; p107 'Water Wars' from 'Water, water everywhere but not a drop to drink' by Paul Brown, *Guardian Education*, 18 March 1997 © The Guardian; p106 'How much do you know about water?' from Youth Topics issue 27 – Water Works, published by CAFOD London, reprinted with permission; p107 'Millions of people still lack safe water' from Tearfund press release reprinted with kind permission of Tearfund UK 2014.